Learning to
LOVE
Later in Life
A Teaching Memoir

James Richard Krum
The Undertaker's Second Son at 87

ISBN: 978-1-09838-557-6 (printed)

ISBN: 978-1-09838-558-3 (eBook)

One who is fearful is half dead.
One who loves is fully alive.

"In the end, only three things matter: how much you loved,
how gently you lived, and how gracefully you let go of things
not meant for you."
The Buddha

"The unexamined life is not worth living."
Socrates

DEDICATION

To Mary Anne Multer, my partner in *learning to love*.

To my children: Carol, Cindy, Cathy, and Jeffrey.

To Margaret, my wife of forty-three years and the mother of our children;
our divorce opened up both of our lives.

OVERVIEW

Gaining freedom from conditioned *behavior* and mastering new ways of *behaving* is the storyline of *Learning to Love Later in Life*. I begin the book by relating the life experiences that established patterns for my behavior in a relationship. As the title reveals, I didn't learn to love until my eighties. The book is based on this definition of learning—the impact of experience on future behavior. If the way to become a proficient driver is to drive, it follows that the way to master love is to practice love. As the subtitle, *A Teaching Memoir,* suggests, you will be instructed periodically to "pause and ponder" how what you are reading relates to your life and later encouraged to design a roadmap to create more love in your life.

TABLE OF CONTENTS

Prologue

In life, most of us get two licenses that open up our world. The first is a driver's license. To qualify, we get a learner's permit and are required to pass a driving test. The second is a marriage license, which does not require a qualifying test. In a heterosexual marriage, a man and a woman are united in holy matrimony, a term that may seem archaic to some readers. In addition to their biologically different *natures,* each partner brings unique life experiences to the altar. These differences in "nature and nurture." create a potentially combustible dynamic if the ability to love is not present. It is likely that unconscious fears and anger lurk below the surface in this mixture. If marriage partners are conscious of the challenge of creating a loving relationship, the inherent differences in *nurture* can be discussed and healed over time. In the same way, the differences in *nature* can be accepted and encouraged. The opposite of acceptance is attempting to change and control one's partner. This memoir explores how the latter dynamic played out in my life and my marriage of forty-three years, which ended in divorce. Fortunately, I found unconditional love in my eighties, and with my new partner, I am learning the complexities of the practice of love.

Foreword: What's Your Point of View?

Taking stock of my life by writing this book has changed me. The careful reader may notice that my perspective on the relative importance of *nature* (genetics) *and nurture* (environment) has changed dramatically from an almost exclusive emphasis on the environment. This change occurred when a friend gave me a book to read that changed my viewpoint. *Blueprint: How DNA Makes Us Who We Are* by Robert Plomin argues convincingly for the critical role that genetics or *nature* plays in our lives.

We all perceive life through a unique set of lenses. Those of us who wear glasses need periodic eye examinations to tell us how accurate our vision is, with 20/20 being the standard. As we age, cataracts and macular degeneration can reduce the clarity of our vision. Surgery and eyeglasses can bring it back to normal for a period of time. And, of course, some people live with varying degrees of blindness.

In a similar way, we perceive life through our unique perspective, point of view, and system of beliefs, and we experience unique emotions. If we are open to examining our lives, our perspective can change over time. This assumes we are also open to change. When I went to college, I carried the perspective I inherited from my father. I was a Lutheran and a conservative Republican. Now, almost seventy years later, I perceive the world through lenses my father could not imagine. Time and events have changed the world, and I have changed with it. I'm now a progressive Democrat and a secular Buddhist. As you will read, my point of view in writing this book was influenced by the insights of the Buddha and New Thought spirituality—Unity and Science of Mind. Rather than being religions with sets of dogma, I view both as complementary philosophies of life. Because both traditions concern understanding the human mind, they also fall into the domain of psychology. Both Buddhism and Science of Mind view "enlightenment" as the highest level of consciousness that a human being can achieve. The rare individual who becomes enlightened has shed his/her self-centered ego and has achieved unconditional love. Five mind states of consciousness (primal, reactive, rational, mystical, and enlightened) are discussed in Chapter 5. You will also encounter these terms in the first three chapters.

Having spent my career in the scholarly world of academia gave me a set of lenses and a unique perspective for viewing the world. My life is dramatically different from that of my sister, Jean, who also grew up "Living Among the Dead" (the topic of the first chapter of the book). In his book, Plomin points out that genetics only makes siblings fifty percent the same. This explains why Jean and I were so different as children. Other than our parents, we have little in common today.

Introduction

This is the story of the life journey of the undertaker's second son. Unlike my older brother, I went to college and graduate school and became a college professor. My older brother went into the family undertaking business, suffered a stroke in his early sixties, and died a wealthy man at sixty-nine. Although I left our apartment above the funeral home behind, the funeral home remains in my psyche to this day. Chapter1, "Living Among the Dead," relates the part of my story that I brought into my marriage. The marriage lasted forty-three years, but was dead for many of those years. My wife, of course, brought her unique childhood experiences and traumas to the marriage. I wish we had realized how poorly prepared we were for marriage at ages twenty-four and twenty-three. Chapter 2 contains reflections on our marriage that produced four wonderful children.

Fifteen years after my divorce, which included two relationships that didn't last, a new woman walked into my life. I was 81; she was 79 and also divorced. As our relationship developed, we decided that we had to *learn how to love*. This led me and Mary Anne to team up to teach "Learning to Love" as a course at Osher Lifelong Learning Institute at the University of Delaware. This book evolved from that course.

In the Table of Contents, you will notice that Chapter 5, "A Roadmap for Creating Love in *Your* Life," is presented as a three-act play; a play suggests action, something you do, not just read about. What it means to be human is the theme of Act 1, "Understanding Yourself," which promotes honest introspection by the reader. It is based upon this wisdom attributed to Socrates: "The unexamined life is not worth living." I might paraphrase it: "The unexamined life is not likely to lead to a successful loving relationship." In short—know yourself and know your partner.

Act 2 picks up when two people enter into a committed relationship and encounter barriers to love. It focuses on ways to confront and, ideally, overcome these barriers. Having brought the funeral home and my unique marital experiences to my new relationship, I came to see my new relationship as a "container" to transform my life from suffering to generosity and love. And, of course, Mary Anne is healing from her unique childhood wounds and experiences in her marriage. When Mary Anne and I became partners, we learned that creating a *conscious* relationship required a commitment to work at it.

Act 3 describes the practice of love. Just as a medical doctor practices his/her profession, becoming proficient at love requires both a commitment to a path and continuous practice. Identifying changes required for creating unconditional love and practicing new behavior is the theme of Act 3, which leads to Chapter 6, "Creating Your Unique Roadmap to Love."

What you are about to read is a memoir, not a textbook. Unlike my life, which will always be a work in progress, a book must freeze time. As you read about my life, I encourage you to look at your own life through new lenses. If you are open to the process of getting to know yourself, I believe your point of view will change as mine has. I encourage you to adopt the goal of becoming more loving as your purpose for reading *Learning to Love Later in Life*.

A Word on Repetition

In the advertising course I taught many years ago, I emphasized the importance of understanding two words—*reach* and *frequency*. Reach emphasizes identifying your target market or audience. In the case of this book, the target audience is people who are searching for love later in their lives. As you know from encountering advertisements in broadcast and print media, repetition is important to get people to act by buying a product or service. Applying the "frequency" principle to this book, you will find many cases where I repeat a message to drive it home.

Before You Begin Reading, Ponder and Write

In a writing course, I learned that a book needs a mystery to keep the reader engaged and turning the pages. As you begin reading my memoir, how do you expect the following questions to be answered: *Is it possible to learn to love? If one does learn to love, will he/she be happy?* Take a few moments to write your answers to these questions and to discuss your reasoning.

Chapter 1:
Living Among the Dead

Preface

Chapter 1 looks at my unusual childhood and adolescent years growing up as part of a business rather than as part of a cohesive family unit. I'm sure you have heard the term 'family business.' However, mine is the story of a *business family*. In essence, my early life was molded to meet the needs of my parents' undertaking business. There were no boundaries between the business and our family and the needs of the business always came first. Being an undertaker is a 24/7/365 commitment. When a call comes in reporting a death, the business springs to action. It's something like a 911 call reporting a fire. A sense of urgency pervaded our family life. This urgency, combined with never having bonded with my mother, whose primary job was managing the office of the business, has festered as a wound my whole life. These two factors had detrimental effects on my being a good husband and father, and were passed on to my children in subtle ways.

When M.B. Met Elsie

Enterprising businessman, widower with two small children, seeks eligible woman with bookkeeping skills and good community contacts.

If newspaper classified personal ads had existed during the mid-1920s, I imagine my father might have written the above advertisement in search of a new wife. M.B. stands for Mizpah Bean, my father's first and middle names. Mizpah comes from the Bible, and Bean was his mother's maiden name. My father was an only child.

Elsie Evans was a good candidate. She came from a large family and was a member of the Lutheran church in the town where M.B. had both his furniture store and his undertaking business. Elsie was a business school graduate. For her, M.B. Krum was a good catch. By temperament, they were opposites. M.B. was a risk-taker who was happiest when he had money borrowed from the bank to expand his business. Elsie kept track of the books and knew how stretched they were financially during the Great Depression when I was born in 1934. I have no idea whether I was planned or not. Being born is one of the few events in my life that I have not had to figure out and manage.

Take Him to the Funeral Home

For many people, their last ride is from the hospital to the funeral home. For me, it was my first ride. Living above the funeral parlor robbed me of my spontaneity and the freedom to be a normal child. I was left in the care of Martha, our live-in housekeeper, who had a large apartment to keep immaculate in addition to doing the cooking and the laundry and taking care of three other children. There was little time for me. As an infant, I must have cried, of course. Eleven years later, when my nephew lived with us as a baby, I can recall my father saying, "Can't you keep that kid quiet?" Early in life, I learned that expressing emotions was not allowed. Eighty-seven years later, my emotions remain bottled up in my body causing anxiety. I still don't cry. However, my anxiety shows up every day in subtle ways. Most mornings, I wake up with it.

As I've tried to understand my infant years, I've envisioned being "abandoned" by my mother when she left me with Martha and walked downstairs to the office of the funeral home which was her comfort zone. When my father's first wife died giving birth to my brother, he hired Martha, a childhood friend, to take care of his two children. Thus, Martha was part of the household before my mother arrived a few years later. As far as I know, the existence of two mother figures in the family was not a source of conflict between them. They each had their role in the business family. If it created a confusing triangle for me, I have no memory of it. Martha became the anchor in my young life. As a youngster, I recall getting up in the middle of the night, walking past my parents' closed bedroom door, through the kitchen to the other side of the apartment. I would go into Martha's room, and say, "Marty, I'm scared." Martha would get up and sit with me until I fell asleep.

Four statements Martha uttered while introducing me to others or putting limits on my behavior have had great impact on my life:

"This is Jimmie; he's the baby of the family."

"This is Jimmie; he's a sickly child."

"This is Jimmie; he's just like his mother. Jean is like M.B."

"Jimmie, you've got to be quiet; there's a funeral on."

All four statements were true. I was younger than my three siblings. While Jean was an extrovert, I was clearly introverted like our mother. I suffered from ear aches until my tonsils were removed when I was about three. Receiving ether to have a tonsillectomy was one of the scariest experiences of my life. It must have been like a near-death experience. I believe the joyous human spirit I was born with gave way to fear when I was three.

While my mother and I lived largely in the world of the business family, M.B.'s life was out in the world, including evenings spent playing cards with his cronies in their clubhouse with its beer cooler. Jean was clearly feistier and out in the world with her friends, like our father. Although we were born three years apart, I have no memories of having her as a playmate as a child.

Dinnertime in Our *Business Family*

We ate dinner in the middle of the day. The seven of us sat around the table in the kitchen. We only ate in the dining room on Sundays. With a funeral scheduled for 1:30, we had to eat and clean up before family and friends of the deceased arrived in the parlor below our apartment. After that, I had to tiptoe around to avoid being heard downstairs.

My father sat at the head of the table in his black suit and tie. To me, my father was larger than life. Although he completed only six years in a one-room schoolhouse plus a short course at embalming school, M.B. purchased the Rohland Funeral Home and with his entrepreneurial genius, personal warmth, and easy laugh, turned it into Lebanon County's leading funeral home. Grayce, my older sister, and my mother sat across the table from my brother, Bob, and me. During the day, the only time I saw my mother was at the dinner table. At the other end of the table, my sister, Jean, and Martha sat across from the patriarch of the family.

If the phone rang during the meal, Elsie would jump up to answer it. Before returning to the table, she would call Charlie and Ed and tell them to go to the hospital to pick up a body. (In my life, *body* remains associated with the word '*dead*'.) Charlie, Ed, and Dick—the men who worked in the business family— were other influences in my young life. Of the three, Charlie was the only one I enjoyed spending time with.

I seldom said anything at the meal table. The conversation of the adults was about the families of the current residents of our hotel for the dead. With the weekly parade of local human-ity through the morgue, slumber rooms, and onto the place of honor in the viewing area, there was never a lack of people to gossip about. If the conversation turned juicy or sensitive, the three adults switched to Pennsylvania Dutch, a form of low German, that I was never encouraged to learn.

At a very young age, I learned that pleasing women (Elsie and Martha) and not upsetting M.B. must be the focus of my life. I learned not to disturb the sensitive balance of our busi-ness family. I became a good boy but somehow lost myself in the process.

The Undertaker's Two Sons

Bob was my half-brother, but I did not know that dis-tinction as we were growing up. He was nine years older than me. Although we shared a bedroom until Bob enlisted in the Navy following Pearl Harbor, I have no memory of us spending time together there. After the war, Bob married his high school sweetheart and went to embalming school. Bob was the "crown prince," always destined to become an undertaker. He walked through life in our father's footsteps, both in the business and in the community. At the age of sixty-one, Bob suffered a stroke and retired before dying of cancer at 69. The last time I visited Bob and his wife in their apartment over the offices of the funeral home, they were sitting in a dark room watching television and smoking. I find it sad that Bob never broke out of our father's shadow and went out to create and live his own life.

At the viewing before his funeral in 1995, I talked to a man who identified himself as Bob's cousin. He said that when he came home from the Navy, Bob told him that he had reservations about becoming an undertaker. However, Bob did what was expected of him. A few years after his stroke, Bob visited me at my cottage in Maine. When I brought up the topic of our childhoods, Bob said, "We had unusual childhoods. I prefer not to think about mine." I'm sure he was referring to growing up as part of the business family.

My contributions to the business began at age five or six. When a funeral was over, my mother would yell, "Ho Jim," up the stairs. This was my cue to go down to the parlor to put the chairs and flower stands away and run the vacuum cleaner. Before graduating from college, I worked at the funeral home during the summers for a total of twelve months. I helped Charlie embalm, dusted or washed the vehicles, and performed various other tasks. When Charlie wanted to teach me to embalm, I declined because I knew I was not cut out to be an undertaker. When I landed a job with Westinghouse Electric Corporation after college, I was finally able to leave the funeral home behind for good. But the funeral home never left me. Recently, it showed up in a dream as I was editing the manuscript of this book.

My Relationship with my Father

While hiking in Maine forty or more years ago, a poem about my late father welled up from my psyche. It began, "This is M.B. Krum, Rohland Funeral Home, they were one and the same," and ended with, "I never knew him." Do any of us really know our parents? At some level, I feared both of my parents. I was afraid to demand their attention. I'm sure I never threw temper tantrums in my childhood. Barry Bricklin, the first of my many psychotherapists beginning in my late thirties and continuing into my eighties, once said, "You give me the impression that you don't deserve to take up space on the planet." That was certainly true of the planet of the Rohland Funeral Home. I believe I emerged from my childhood with a great deal of repressed fear and anger about having my emotions as well as my human spirit squelched.

When I was in high school, my father offered to buy me a Cadillac convertible if I would agree to go to embalming school and go into the family business. As I look back on the arc of my life, deciding to go to college instead of embalming school was a departure from living my father's dream that I would spend my life taking care of the dead. Becoming an undertaker would have been a waste of my talents and I would have been unhappy working for my father.

After college, I worked at Westinghouse Electric for fourteen months before deciding to go to graduate school to pursue a master's degree in business administration. An opportunity to teach as a graduate assistant opened a new career path to me. Writing a master's thesis, I found that I enjoyed research and had a knack for it. When a senior faculty member described himself as a scholar as well as a teacher, a new perspective opened for me. I went on to earn a doctorate in business administration

(D.B.A.) and spent thirty-five years teaching in a college and a university. During that period, I spent five years as chair of a large academic department. When my term expired, I was happy to escape the stress of academic administration.

In writing this book, I've come to realize I am much more like my father than my mother. My father was an entrepreneur who created a successful business, which as you will see, was sold for millions of dollars after my brother died. But that is getting ahead of the story. As a college professor, I was a change agent like my father. I was the driving force behind updating our undergraduate and graduate programs. I conducted research in England and taught courses in Bulgaria where I wrote a book that was published in Bulgarian. Although our careers could not have been more different, my father and I were both progressives in our fields.

Growing up with a largely absent father and being branded by Martha as being just like my mother took a toll on my masculinity. Being raised in a family environment totally devoid of any expressions of intimacy took a toll on my sexuality. Both factors played out in my adolescent years and influenced the kind of husband and father I became. Being raised in a patriarchal family, but not being a patriarch by temperament, I failed to understand the importance of a father in the lives of my three daughters. I regret this and am proud of my connection to them today. On the plus side, I spent a lot of time with my son, something my father never did with me.

Growing up over the funeral home stole my childhood. I believe I should be compensated for that. This takes us to the next two sections, which concern my current energy toward my sister.

The Meeting in the Casket Room

A month after my brother's funeral, Marlyn Gohn, my brother-in-law, called to invite me to a meeting of the stockholders of the funeral home to act on its sale to a national corporation. This was my first stockholders' meeting since my father gave me a few shares before he died in 1970. On the day of the meeting, Marlyn greeted me in the office and told me that everyone else was assembled in the casket room. I walked with Marlyn through the empty funeral parlor as I had thousands of times before, and up the stairs to the casket display room above the garage and morgue. As the place where the profits of the business originated, the casket room was a fitting place to dispose of it. In marketing terms, the casket room was the sales office.

When I entered the room, the other stockholders were seated around a large table with several cremation urns serving as centerpieces. I took my seat with a display of twenty or so caskets behind me. In addition to Marlyn, my sister, Jean, and my brother's widow (also named Jean), the group included two employees—licensed funeral directors, who had purchased stock at book value over the years. One of them was Dick Basselgia, who had been a part of the business as long as I can remember.

I had grown up in the closed system of the funeral home and its employees. As a child, Dick frequently sent me across the street to buy him a pack of cigarettes. I recall with satisfaction the day I told him to go buy his own cigarettes. Although I didn't care for Dick, I am indebted to him for one thing. When I was four or five, I took a puff from one of his cigarettes that I found in an ashtray and became sick. I never tried a cigarette again in my life. Thank you, Dick.

Marlyn introduced an attorney from Harrisburg who began a lengthy description of the proposed sale of the business. As I listened, a number of things became obvious to me. First, my father's stock had been sold over the years to the principals in the business with my brother getting the largest share. Stock had also been sold to the two non-family members who were seated at the table. It became apparent to me that I was the only person at the table who had not benefited from purchasing funeral home stock at book value (which was considerably below market value). I also learned that over and above the value of the stock that Marlyn owned, he would receive a substantial sum for agreeing not to compete with the new owners, something I'm sure he had no intention of doing. He and my sister, who never worked in the business, would become wealthy. In comparison, I would receive meager compensation from the sale of the business that had such a profound influence on my childhood.

My thoughts turned to the impact the proposed sale of the business would have on my parents' nine grandchildren. Only three of the nine—Bob's daughter and Jean and Marlyn's two daughters—were likely to eventually inherit money. My four children would, in effect, receive nothing. My sense of fairness was violated. I said so and refused to sign the document authorizing the sale.

When I raised my objection, the lawyer explained that if all shareholders did not sign the papers he had prepared for the meeting, he would have to go to court to allow the sale without all of the signatures. For the first time in my life, I thought I had some leverage in the family.

I proposed that those who had benefited from buying stock at substantially below market price sell some of their shares to me and to my late sister Grayce's husband. This would achieve a more equitable benefit of the sale for my parents' grandchildren. What I saw as a reasonable proposal was met with dead silence, appropriate for the setting. In essence, the participants in the meeting, including my sister and sister-in-law, preferred to spend money on lawyers and court costs and delay the process rather than allowing it to benefit all of the founder's grandchildren, including the only male heir to take the Krum name into the next generation. That continuation of the family surname was important to the founder of the business.

I refused to sign. Speaking through an electronic voice box following surgery for throat cancer, Dick croaked, "The old man should never have given him stock." After stewing for several days, I decided to sign the papers and asked Marlyn to send them to me. Maintaining a relationship with Jean, my only remaining blood relative, was more important than my feeling of being cheated out of my birthright and receiving compensation for my lost childhood living above the funeral home.

Twenty-five Years Later

During an exercise in a workshop twenty-five years after the meeting in the casket room, I realized that I was still carrying anger toward my sister. After recognizing this previously repressed emotion, I decided to write a letter asking Jean and Marlyn to correct what I considered to be a gross unfairness in the distribution of the millions of dollars from the sale of the funeral home. In the letter, I told Jean that I didn't want to live the rest of my life carrying anger toward her and also carrying fear about my children's welfare after I died. I reminded Jean that I received little inheritance when our parents died in their seventies because all of their money was tied up in the business.

I also told her that my estate would be modest because of my divorce. Knowing that her two daughters are "well-off," I proposed that some of the money Jean and Marlyn received from the sale of the business be used to establish a trust for the benefit of my children with any remaining balance going to Jean and Marlyn's grandchildren.

I did not receive a response to possibly the most important letter I have ever written. Twenty days after writing the letter, I sent Jean a second one that was also ignored. About three weeks later, I received what I consider to be a condescending letter from Marlyn, essentially telling me to "bug off." A few weeks later, I received a letter from my sister's two daughters saying that their parents had shared my letters with them. Their letter said, "You are causing our mother much sorrow and anxiety." In response, I told my nieces that my cascade of letters[1] would have been avoided if their mother had honored my concerns with a response to my first letter.

Being ignored by my sister brought up rage that I did not know was buried in my body since my childhood, when I felt marginalized by the family. This anger first came out more than forty years ago after our mother fell and required hip replacement surgery. When my brother and sister planned to follow the doctor's advice and send her to an inner-city hospital in Harrisburg for rehabilitation, I visited a facility in rural Lancaster county that was run by Mennonite women. This facility was culturally a better fit for our mother, who was a private person. But I was overruled by my two siblings, who took her to the Harrisburg facility. The orderlies there were men who, according to her roommate, dropped her on the floor on one occasion. When I confronted a hospital administrator, he

---

1 My computer file contains ten letters I wrote over a four-month period.

denied it. As I recall, male orderlies took her to a shower room. I don't believe my mother ever took a shower in her life; she always took baths. The rehab hospital experience was an affront to our mother's dignity and undoubtedly left a scar more serious than a replaced hip. My brother and sister never apologized for ignoring my recommendation and putting our mother in that situation.

As I ponder my difference from my only biological sibling, I believe Jean is frozen in time and place. She never left the culture of the funeral home behind as I did. I doubt that the concepts of learning to love and becoming transformed have any meaning for her. Although her life may have been enjoyable, it was shallow by my standards. But, "different strokes for different folks." I'm sure my sister sees me as being too introspective. Although we share the same parents, we were born with dramatically different temperaments, and our life journeys could not have been more different. Living in a college environment, I became a liberal Democrat. But never leaving our hometown, I believe Jean remained a conservative Republican like our father. I doubt that generosity is one of Jean's values. Instead, she lives in a world of winners and losers.

Recently, at 4:30 in the morning I received an intuitive message to open my heart to my sister. That message from my subconscious moved me to write a letter to Jean and Marlyn, apologizing for my angry letters and asked them to forgive me. Jean responded with a kind note that ended with "I wish I could erase your anger." After drafting a long response about why I deserved a share in the wealth from the sale of the funeral home, I read it to my daughter, Carol, who said, "That sounds like a victim story to me." After acknowledging that it was, I wrote a note to Jean asking her to talk sister-to-brother. As I was writing the note, it occurred to me that Jean has her own victim story. I believe she was envious of my career that included numerous trips to Europe, a decade of summer camping trips, and a cottage in Maine while her family was tied down with Marlyn running the funeral home. This insight gave me some empathy for her position. After not receiving a response from my request that we communicate as siblings, I wrote the following letter to Jean.

July 28, 2020

Dear Jean,

Using a divorce term, it's obvious to me that you and I have "irreconcilable differences." Our life paths could not have been more different. You never left the shadow of the RFH. I traveled through the academic world, became a liberal Democrat, and later a Buddhist. As a result of our different life experiences, our worldviews and values seem to be diametrically opposed. I believe in win-win and you seem to believe in winners and losers. Other than sharing a mother, we have little in common and my attempts to communicate became painful for both of us.

For me, it's time to lead our own lives with no pretense of having a meaningful connection with each other. We don't need stress at this point in our lives.

I wish you well, Jean.

Love,

Jim

I thought that letter ended a painful chapter in my life. However, five months after writing it, I received a Christmas card from my sister. On December 25th, I called Jean to wish her a merry Christmas. Two months later Jean called to wish me a happy birthday.

As I ponder these events that occurred a year ago, I wonder what roles Jean's husband and her daughter (who manages their finances) played in her decision to ignore my letters. It's not likely that I will ever know. As I'm writing, Jean will soon turn ninety.

My Funeral Home

My father died in 1970, a half century ago. After his funeral, my mother gave me a basket of flowers to take home. I recall placing the flowers on our dining room table and taking pictures of my wife, Margaret, sitting next to them. When we were decorating our house three years earlier, I had insisted on having a curtain hung on the back wall of the dining room to cover the door to the screen porch. Seventeen years after taking those pictures of Margaret, I realized that by hanging those curtains, I had subconsciously created my own funeral home. I had created a space like a viewing room to pay respects to the deceased.

With this realization twenty years after installing the curtains, I organized Cathy and Jeffrey, two of our children, to do a thorough house cleaning while Margaret was at her ashram. (As will be explained later, by this point in our marriage, Margaret was devoted to a Hindu guru.) In the process, we removed the heavy curtains in the dining room and living room and moved a dump truck load of accumulated junk to the front yard for the city to pick up. Over a weekend, we both cleansed the house of many memories and lightened its "feel"—it was no longer *my* funeral home. But Margaret was less than pleased when she returned home. Unfortunately, in the cleaning process, we threw out a box of Margaret's mother's recipes. I believe she felt invaded.

Postscript: A Fuller Perspective on my Childhood

Although I may have felt abandoned as a child, I do not want to imply that I was not wanted or deliberately neglected. It's just that nobody had time for me. I did not lack material support. A framed set of three studio portraits of me taken when I was six or seven months old verifies that I was valued.

For a child born during depths of the Great Depression, with the success of the undertaking business, my life was privileged in material ways. Before the advent of public kindergartens, I was enrolled in a private one. We had a summer cottage until World War II. In our attic, we had a pool table where I entertained my friends. When I needed a suit to wear to church, my mother took me to the best men's clothing store in town; as I recall, my first suit had knickers. I trusted my parents and they trusted me. When I received my driver's license, I had the use of the family Buick to pal around with my three high school buddies.

Although the word 'love' was never used, my parents and Martha clearly cared about me. Being the youngest of four children, I don't recall spending much time with my three siblings who had their own friends and lives outside of our home. I became a loner. I recall spending a lot of time in my bedroom listening to a small radio that was my cherished companion. As for extended family, I never knew either of my grandmothers. As noted earlier, my mother's mother died when she was born.

My sense is that my father also lost his mother during his child-hood and was raised by his father.

Chapter 2:
Reflections on My Forty-Three Year Marriage

Preface

Margaret brought her anger toward men to our marriage, and I carried an unconscious fear of women and also fear of my sexuality. My healthy, biological *nature* had been squelched in my childhood. This combination of fear and anger played havoc with our sex life, which was seldom satisfying for either of us. In romance novels, sexual intercourse is an enjoyable act of love. However, speaking as a man, fear can overwhelm the experience if one's partner is not satisfied; at that point, sex becomes a performance to meet expectations. Although I sired four children, I never experienced an orgasm. While doing "men's work" later in life, I learned the distinction between ejaculation and an orgasm. I was too controlled to let go and experience the latter.

Years into our marriage, I sometimes invited Margaret to attend a psychotherapy session with me. In one session, my therapist told us: "Margaret feels like a bird in a cage and you are her jailer." I never did unlock the cage. Out of fear of rejection, I became passive-aggressive when she managed to break out and find meaning in her life by becoming devoted to a Hindu guru.

Thus, fear and anger dominated our marriage that lasted forty-three years. The last two decades existed in name only. Recognizing my fear and largely passive-aggressive anger as well as Margaret's anger toward men raises the question of whether

Margaret was afraid of me. That question was answered when we attempted divorce mediation and Margaret was silent during the first and only session. When I asked her "why" as we were driving home, Margaret said, "I can't stand up to you." Having learned to control myself as an infant, I believe I covered my insecurity and anxiety by controlling situations (and others) to the best of my ability. As a result of this dynamic, when one of my therapists met Margaret and observed us together, he remarked, "You two don't connect." He was right.

Overview

In the spring of my senior year of college, I faced the prospect of returning to life above the funeral home after several interviews did not result in a job offer. As I was walking across the campus one afternoon, I encountered Dr. William O. Duck, the Gettysburg College placement director, who told me that a representative of Westinghouse Electric Corporation had showed up unannounced and he needed students to talk to him. Without time to go back to the fraternity house to put on my suit and tie, I went to the interview and was offered a job, which I started six weeks later in Pittsburgh. Thus, being in the right place at the right time (divine order?) determined the trajectory for the rest of my life and the birth of four children.

At Westinghouse, a colleague told me that he and his wife had a college friend named Margaret they wanted me to meet. That blind date eventually led to my first kiss—at Margaret's initiative—since seventh grade.

After I left Westinghouse to pursue my master's degree, Margaret and I stayed in touch. Following a three-month engagement, we married a year and a half after we met. Looking back, we hardly knew each other or ourselves. As you will see, we had four children during the first seven years of our marriage. But our marriage never gelled for reasons discussed in the preface.

After a challenging four-decade marriage, Margaret and I decided to divorce and told our children. By that point, our oldest daughter had dropped out of our lives. Carol had "divorced" her mother and later me, after she told us about an incident with her uncle that is described in a later section. Shortly after the decision to end our marriage, I was diagnosed with prostate cancer. Walking to my office one day, I realized that I couldn't handle divorce and prostate cancer at the same time; we abandoned plans to divorce. When I retired two years later, it was obvious that Margaret had developed her own life as a Reiki Master (teacher) and devotee of her guru. For all intents and purposes, the marriage was dead. Moving to a co-housing community in North Carolina did not save our marriage. We divorced three years after that move.

A Traumatic Sexual Experience I Brought to the Marriage

I had an experience in eighth grade that impacted the next ten years of my life and affected my marriage. In seventh grade, as I was approaching puberty, I had a girlfriend named Susan (name changed). We went to parties where spin the bottle was part of our rites of passage. During the spring following my thirteenth birthday, Susan and I went on several hayrides where we snuggled up in the corner of the wagon and "necked." I took Susan to the seventh-grade dance in the junior high school gymnasium.

By eighth grade, my healthy development yielded to forces beyond my control. I was beginning to have wet dreams. In school, I became jealous when I saw Susan talking to other boys. And then a life-changing event occurred. At half-time of an afternoon junior varsity football game, a group of us were hanging out in the nearly empty grandstand when Susan came over and sat on my lap. I slowly developed an erection that went up the side of Susan's leg. Neither of us said anything or reacted in any way. As I look back on this seminal experience in my relationship with women, I was both mortified and ashamed by this uncontrollable physical expression. Having never discussed it, I don't know how Susan felt. After that incident, fear led me to withdraw from dating. When I saw Susan at our sixtieth high school class reunion, I asked her if I could give her a hug. After I did, Susan said, "That's the first time you hugged me since seventh grade."

Although I had a handful of "dates" in high school and college, I did not kiss a female again until I met my future wife. In essence, I was afraid of my sexuality, and have never felt fully comfortable with it. Sexual incompatibility affected our marriage and undoubtedly contributed to our divorce. My wife brought her own issues concerning sexuality to our marriage. She had been sexually abused as a teenager as well as shortly before we met.

Why did this event become a big deal that continues to haunt my life? Growing up over the funeral home, my life had been about self-control. But suddenly there was a part of my anatomy that I could not control and I became afraid of it. During my marriage, this anxiety played out in premature ejaculations resulting in our dysfunctional sex life.

The term 'sexual repression' was coined by Sigmund Freud, who viewed it as the chief psychological problem in society. It's curious that my decades of psychotherapy for anxiety and depression largely ignored what I now see as my repressed sexuality. Becoming impotent since cryosurgery for prostate cancer more than twenty years ago was a welcome relief for me.

I Married a Family

Family systems theory explains how each of us is a product of our family of origin. You have read the story of the impact that growing up over the funeral home had on my life. And Margaret brought her own childhood wounds to the marriage. Both of Margaret's parents emigrated from Scotland. Her father was a successful plumbing contractor, and her mother, whom I loved, stayed at home and never learned to drive.

During her childhood, Margaret lost two siblings: a sister to an illness and a brother, who was playing with gasoline and matches with his friends and burned to death. These deaths cast a shadow on the family. Her father clearly favored Margaret's two remaining brothers, especially his youngest son, who went on to receive three degrees from M.I.T. Favoring the male line was typical of patriarchal families. Although Margaret was highly intelligent, her father squelched her desire to become a medical doctor by telling her that "women are not doctors." As noted in the preface, I believe Margaret brought a lot of resentment and anger toward men to our marriage.

What I am going to say next is hard for me to write, but it can't be avoided. As an adult, Carol recalled and wrote about memories of being sexually abused by her uncle, beginning as a preschooler. As I have reflected on the accusation, I found it credible to believe that Margaret's oldest brother, now deceased, was a pedophile who stole our daughter's innocence. When Carol's stories of abuse came to light years later, "Where was I?" was the question I had to wrestle with. My best answer is that

I must have been drinking heavily with my brother-in-law and was fast asleep.

More importantly, I was not aware of the need to protect my daughter from a relative, a man who was to become her legal guardian in our will, if something happened to my wife and me. A few years after Carol's accusations, Margaret recalled being abused by the same brother, a memory she had repressed since she was a teenager. Later, being concerned about the safety of her brother's grandchildren, Margaret wrote a letter to his wife and three children accusing him of being a pedophile. In response, he denied her accusation and cut off communication with her until she retracted it. Margaret never retracted the accusations made in her letter.

Our Honeymoon

Margaret and I married when I was twenty-four and a graduate student. The wedding was in the Presbyterian church that Margaret attended. My brother was my best man. Our parents "hit it off" and we later learned that there was quite a party at Margaret's house following the reception and our departure on our honeymoon.

When we got to the motel room to spend our first night together, I suggested that we take a walk around town. I was scared, but as a man, could not admit that to myself or to my bride, who was probably also scared. Being inexperienced, my rational mind (which ran my life) had no idea what to do, and my primal mind had been obliterated early in my childhood. As I reflect, if my wife and I had been able to admit and discuss our ignorance and fear, the honeymoon and marriage might have turned out better. But neither of us had experience acknowledging and/or talking about our feelings. I figured sex out, and sixteen months later, became a father. This transition to fatherhood was even scarier than our honeymoon.

"Little Jimmie" Becomes a Father

Margaret and I married between the two years of my master's program. After receiving my degree, I took a job as an instructor at Gettysburg College, three years and three months after graduating from the school. As the first semester was drawing to a close, I was adjusting to being married, playing college professor, teaching courses I was poorly qualified to teach, and my wife was expecting a baby. I was in way over my head. Extremely stressed, I somehow managed to make it through the first four months of the semester as the due date of the baby approached.

In mid-December, I felt faint in class one morning. I dismissed the class and walked home. Being overcome with fear, I believed I would have a heart attack if I walked downstairs from our third-floor apartment. I lay around all day; Margaret somehow managed to cope with me. After a doctor examined me and assured me that there was nothing organically wrong with my health and with the baby due in mid-January, I told Margaret that I wanted to go "home" to celebrate Christmas with my family.

On Christmas Eve, we went to a party at the home of my sister, Grayce. Her husband served an alcoholic punch, and I made numerous trips to the punch bowl in order to soothe my anxiety. During the party, Margaret's water broke. She had to explain to me what that meant. Although I was feeling the alcohol, I drove the few blocks back to the funeral home and went to bed to sleep off the effects of the alcohol. At about 2 a.m. I drove Margaret to the hospital where Dr. Groh, my childhood doctor, had agreed to deliver the baby. Sadly, Margaret met this rather gruff doctor for the first time in the delivery room. Because of her understandable nervousness, Dr. Groh gave Margaret anesthesia to put her to sleep. After waiting for three of the longest hours of my life, I learned that I was the father of a healthy baby girl. Because of me, this was hardly a natural welcome into the world for our daughter or a joyous moment for her mother.

When I went to see Dr. Groh after Margaret and Carol came home from the hospital, he examined me and referred me to a psychiatrist, who told me that I had experienced a severe panic attack (in lay terms, a nervous breakdown). With the help of tranquilizers (drugs that reduce anxiety), I managed to return to teaching after the Christmas break, and four years later, went on to earn my doctorate.

Unfortunately, I lacked the maturity to be a father. I had no concept of the requirements of fatherhood and lacked a model in my father. But that didn't stop us from having three more children in the next six and a half years, two of whom were born in Michigan, where I was in graduate school. Having and raising children dominated our lives while I finished graduate school and began the process of earning tenure at the University of Delaware, where I taught for thirty-one years.

Parenting

In retrospect, having four children during the first seven years of our marriage was insane. None of them were planned and I was either struggling at "playing" college professor or working toward my doctorate when they were born. With the exception of Martha and Margaret's mother, we lacked role models for loving parenting.

Margaret and I shared major decisions in creating opportunities for our young family. The first, which Margaret initiated, was enrolling Cindy and Cathy (and later Jeff) in a new
alternative private school, Newark Center for Creative Learning
(NCCL). I believe this was a life-changing decision for Cindy,
as was a second one initiated by her mother. After NCCL, when
Cindy had trouble adapting to public high school, Margaret
read about the Trailside Country School, which traveled the
country on a bus. Cindy's two years in the program contributed
greatly to creating her life path. Cathy was the middle child
caught between two older sisters and her brother who required
a lot of attention. To bring meaning to her life, we bought Cathy
a horse that she stabled and rode at a nearby state park.

Although Jeff had a good foundation at the university pre-
school and kindergarten, he struggled with learning to read in
the first grade. When we had him evaluated by a psychologist, a
new word—dyslexia—entered our vocabularies. This led us to
apply for and receive full state funding for him to attend various private schools from the fifth grade onwards. When we
exhausted resources in Delaware, the state paid for Jeff to attend
private schools for dyslexics in Wisconsin and Massachusetts.
The funding breakthrough came when I learned of U.S. Law
94-142, which guarantees every student a free and appropriate
education. To get the funding for Jeff, we argued successfully
that special education programs in the public schools failed to
understand the needs of students with dyslexia, a specific learning disability, and thus lacked programs to remediate it.

Carol missed the opportunity to attend NCCL because
she was too old when the school opened. After college, Carol
learned about Reiki healing and began to study it. When she
wanted to become a Reiki Master, Margaret and I paid the
$10,000 fee for her to be trained and initiated by the Grand

Master. Becoming a Reiki Master created a sense of direction in Carol's life. In her sixties, practicing and teaching Reiki remains at the core of her life. For years, Carol has been a lesbian.

As I look back, becoming a father led to the most satisfying accomplishments in my life. I treasure my relationships with each of my children today. After I retired, I read about 'generativity' and adopted it as the core philosophy for my retirement years. The term, coined by psychologist Erik Erickson, contends that people my age have a choice—they can either stagnate or become generative and use their wisdom and resources to lay a foundation for the next generation. I'm pleased to be able to assist my children financially in economic times that are more challenging than when I became an adult. Being a product of the low birth rate during the years of the Great Depression, I graduated from college into the booming economy of the 1950s. In comparison, our children were born during the years of the baby boom and reached maturity during a much more difficult economic landscape. Under these conditions, we may have misguided our children by encouraging them to adopt Joseph Campbell's admonition to "follow your bliss". It might have been more helpful to tell them, "It's a tough world out there".

Over the years, various comments from our adult children raised the question of whether we were too trusting and even oblivious as parents. Did we sometimes give our children more freedom than they could handle rather than offering guidance and setting boundaries for them? In retrospect, I'm sure the answer is *yes*. Being preoccupied with work, I took a *laissez-faire* approach to parenting and was out of touch with a rapidly changing culture that led to the use of alcohol and illegal drugs by our children.

Reflecting on his early life, recently Jeffrey asked me, "Why didn't you punish me when I got caught by authorities using alcohol?" I didn't have a good answer to his question. The good news is that all four of our children managed to weather the storms of adolescence.

Regrets as a Parent

As a parent, I have two major regrets. The following excerpt from a poem by Carol demonstrates how unaware I was as a father. The poem relates to abuse by her uncle.

"But I was just a child"

I scream

"They were supposed to protect me."

The poem was written by Carol in 1992, the year she turned thirty-three and decided to divorce her parents. In her thirties, Carol, the oldest of my three daughters, had memories of the sexual abuse by her uncle and later by other men. I had her poems in the drawer of my bedside table for fifteen years, but until recently, failed to ponder them.

As a parent, my greatest regret is not protecting Carol from sexual abuse. About the time I retired, Carol dropped out of the family and legally changed her name. I never saw my oldest child for more than a decade, during which she was healing from the traumatic experiences of sexual abuse in her childhood. Living simply in a tiny house without plumbing that she built, Carol is thriving today.

My other regret is that my use of alcohol created a poor role model for my children. When the kids were in their late twenties and thirties, I wrote them a letter asking them what they remembered about me as a father. Drinking was one common element in the four answers I received. If I could live my life over, I would not have started drinking when I was in college.

At eighty-seven, I have a good relationship with my three daughters. However, my relation with Jeff is sometimes challenging, and as I reflect, has been for much of his life. Jeff is married and lives in Florida. Having had several surgeries on his back and knee, Jeff lives in constant physical pain that is controlled by prescription painkillers. Because of his disabilities, Jeff's world as he approaches fifty-six is quite limited. Walking is difficult for him.

Our conflicts over the years seem to result from my inability to be the person Jeff wants me to be. And vice versa, I guess. University of Delaware sports, especially football, are Jeff's passions. We had season tickets for football and basketball games while Jeff was growing up. As I'm writing this, the Delaware women's basketball team is competing for a national championship. A few days ago, Jeff called and urged me to watch their game. When I told Jeff that I'm no longer interested in Delaware sports, he was crushed and used an expletive causing me to hang up on him. The way this conversation ended felt like a punch in my gut; I imagine Jeff felt the same way. Over the years, we have experienced periodic flare-ups like this one.

Using the book *Opening Up by Writing It Down*,[2] I decided to write about my feelings. As the words flowed onto paper in three fifteen-minute writing sessions, I realized that it was time to enlist a family therapist to help Jeff and me to discuss our relationship. During a virtual session with Jeff and me, the therapist urged us to let go of the past and create a new relationship

---

2 Pennebaker, James W. and Joshua M. Smyth, *Opening Up by Writing It Down* (New York: The Guilford Press, 2016).

that can become a rewarding connection for both of us. I now see that accepting Jeff where he is today is the loving thing to do. Having said that, I believe letting go of patterns established over almost six decades will be a challenge for me and also for Jeff. Consistent with my philosophy of generativity, learning to love each of my children in new ways that serve them is my new commitment. Therefore, to relate to Jeff, I plan to rekindle my interest in Delaware sports.

Creating caring children was our greatest accomplishment as parents. As their mother is dying, our children support each other via conference calls and by texting. As Jeff is facing another surgery on his knee, he sent this text to his sisters: "This is going to be a hard time for me. [After the surgery] I would like to hear all three of your voices. I think it will help me." Carol responded, "I hear you. Sending hugs." And Cathy followed up with, "It is understandable to be scared. Will try to help you get through it." What a family!

Grandparenting

Margaret and I have two grandchildren—Cathy's son, Alex, and Cindy's daughter, Anya. In Chapter 3, you will read how important being one of Anya's caregivers was in healing from my divorce. After spending six years helping take care of her, I feel a real bond with Anya. I regret that I don't have a similar connection with Alex. When he was a preschooler, I was impressed with how curious Alex was about the world around him.

After thriving at Newark Center for Creative Learning, Alex attended a highly rated, but regimented, charter high school where he was enrolled in a STEM (science, technology, engineering, mathematics) curriculum. The transition from a less structured to a highly structured educational setting was difficult for Alex, and I believe it killed his desire to learn. Rather than being enjoyable, learning became a chore.

After high school, Alex was admitted to the College of Engineering at the University of Delaware. As a result of the "sink or swim" philosophy of teaching freshmen in the College of Engineering, Alex withdrew after one semester, feeling demoralized and disillusioned with higher education. Based on Alex's experience, I lost my esteem for the University where I taught for thirty-one years. In my mind, it's unconscionable for a freshman program to employ a sink or swim philosophy that fails to properly teach students how to swim. Alex remains unclear about what he wants to do in life. I'm confident that Alex will find a path where he can use his considerable abilities and find meaning in his life. I believe cars and gaming, whatever that is, are his passions at this time.

Anya's primary education was at a small Quaker school in Maine and a charter school in Hawaii. She had a mixed experience in secondary education. When she lived in Hawaii, she thrived in the private Hawaiian School for Girls. Anya then attended a public high school when her father got a job in Maine. She did well academically there, but found it challenging to fit in socially as a transfer student. During a gap year between high school and college, the Covid-19 pandemic brought a young man into her life, and they wound up traveling and hiking together for five months.

Anya plans to study sustainable agriculture at the University of Massachusetts online. To combat global warming, Anya envisions the Hawaiian Islands growing most of their own food rather than importing it. As she is about to turn twenty, my granddaughter seems to have a clear vision and sense of purpose in her life; she is wise beyond her years. Her mother's life work in protecting the environment and her father's passion for writing have blossomed in Anya.

I bought a smart phone and am learning to use it in order to keep in touch with my granddaughter. To me, she is "Amazing Anya."

Beginning Psychotherapy

Twelve years into our marriage, my career was well established. I was no longer in survival mode after three years as a doctoral student and four years earning tenure at the University of Delaware. By this time, our children had gone off to school, and with an empty nest, Margaret was searching for meaning in her life beyond being the wife of a college professor. In the context of the women's movement of the 1970s, I realized that I needed to pay more attention to my marriage.

Three events happened during this period that changed my life. The first was a weekend workshop based on the Thomas Harris book, *I'm OK, You're OK*, that Margaret and I attended. After the workshop, I focused on my marriage instead of my career for the first time. A few years later, a second event shook me to my core. When Margaret had an appointment for counseling with the new associate minister at our Presbyterian church, he invited her to join him in sponsoring a youth group he was forming. With a stale marriage, Margaret became infatuated with another man for the first time. She showed her affection by rushing up to hug him after church services. In our relationship, Margaret and I had never hugged. I was dumbstruck by a situation I had never contemplated.

The third event occurred when I was asked by the wife of the senior minister to join her in teaching an adult church school class on the book, *Honest to God,* by Anglican Bishop John A.T. Robinson. Reading this book shook my belief in God as will be discussed in Chapter 5. Within a period of a few years, my marriage was threatened and my belief in the "God" of my Lutheran upbringing was destroyed. Consequently, I left the church and became an agnostic. Our children followed me out the door; but Margaret stayed and worked with the associate minister in developing a creative celebration at 9:30 on Sunday mornings as an alternative to the more traditional church service at 11:00.

As these events played out, Margaret and I decided it was time to get marriage counseling. When I called the therapist that a neighbor recommended, he asked, "Is there another man involved?" I told him about Margaret's infatuation with the associate minister and scheduled an appointment. After seeing Margaret and me together a few times, the therapist told us that he had to deal with our individual issues before he could work with us on the marriage. This led to weekly individual appointments that lasted about three months until Margaret dropped out because she was convinced that I was the problem. However, I continued. If Margaret had been willing to look at her own issues, I believe our marriage might have turned out differently.

This was the beginning of more than four decades of psychotherapy, almost all of which was paid for by my medical insurance. Years ago, a friend described psychotherapy as my addiction of choice. I learned a lot about myself during these weekly sessions. However, if I were starting therapy today, I would look for a therapist who recognized the importance of the more holistic mind-body connection. "How do you feel about that?" was seldom asked in a therapy session. As a result, buried emotions of fear, sadness, and anger were seldom probed in the fifty-minute sessions.

After being introduced to Siddha Yoga by a friend, Margaret stopped going to the Presbyterian church, ending that difficult phase of my life. Finding a guru dramatically changed Margaret's life, as she began spending more and more time at her guru's ashram several hours away. Over the years, as her absences from our home increased, I became resentful and my anger about the situation sizzled. When Margaret returned from her frequent trips, I can't imagine her wanting to come home--to me--a passive-aggressive husband.

Warriors of the Heart and Lifespring

During this period of profound change in my life, I completed my five-year term as Chairman of the Department of Business Administration. One evening, as Margaret was preparing dinner, I went through the mail (probably with a glass of Scotch and water in my hand) and came upon a flier announcing the introduction to a program named 'Warriors of the Heart' at a local church. Because Margaret was already on her spiritual journey, I decided to attend by myself, but at the last-minute invited Margaret to join me. We went together and the weekend workshop led to a residential retreat a few weeks later.

When Margaret and I attended the retreat, our marriage was coming apart; we were living parallel lives. Margaret was enjoying and guarding her independence at a time when I was looking forward to more time together following my freedom from administrative responsibilities. Without going into detail, our drama played out during the retreat. On the final morning, most of the thirty participants were sharing their good feelings with the group while I sat in the back silently brooding. As the sharing period was ending, I raised my hand, and said, "I want to be healed." Daanan Parry, the workshop facilitator, asked all the men to come to the center of the circle to pick me up and cradle me. As I look back, being cradled by men was the beginning of a new chapter in my life. When they put me down, I felt transformed. I recall Margaret crying and being comforted by the women.

Friends we met at the Warriors of the Heart weekend introduced us to the Lifespring Trainings that Margaret and I enrolled in two months later. I was ripe for a breakthrough—and had one. When I completed the Lifespring Advanced Training, I felt like I had blown my mind; for a few weeks, I was not living in my head. I felt free and was able to be more present. My normal anxious, introverted behavior was gone. I recall being in a gift store in Bar Harbor, Maine, and relating to the saleslady as another human being, not simply as the lady in the role she was playing. It seemed that my heart had opened to other people. I came out of the training less inhibited and with more zest for life.

Founded in 1974, the Lifespring Trainings (basic, advanced, and leadership program) followed Erhard Seminar Training (est) which began in 1971. Both were part of the human potential or large group awareness movement of that period of dramatic social change. I did the *est* training in 1981 and the Lifespring Basic and Advanced Trainings in 1987. Although they were similar, Lifespring was kinder and gentler and had a profound influence on my life. Even though this freer way of being faded over time, I realized that dramatic change is possible. Eventually, my anxiety returned, but I now had a renewed perspective on my life.

During this period, Margaret and I communicated more openly about issues in our marriage. In the beginning of the Lifespring Basic Training, the trainer challenged us to look at the routines or ruts we had dug that inhibited changing our lives. During the basic training, I learned that I could dance without feeling foolish and also learned the lift that comes from hugging both women and men. Going through the "hug-line" was a powerful experience for me.

At the beginning of the advanced training, the facilitator pulled Margaret and me aside and told us that our marriage might not survive the training. Having completed question-naires before the advanced training, Margaret apparently revealed aspects of her life that I knew nothing about. We agreed to continue with the training. After completing it, I boiled the advanced training down to the word 'integrity'—the quality of being honest and having strong moral principles.

As we were driving to our cottage in Maine after the advanced training, Margaret told me that she was out of integrity in our marriage. Ouch! At that time more than three decades ago, I lacked the ability to understand her perspective and viewed what she proceeded to tell me through self-centered lenses. Rather than having empathy for my wife, I judged her. Now, three decades later, I believe I understand where she was coming from and regret that I didn't handle the difficult situation for my wife in a loving way. I lacked compassion for my wife's struggles with our marriage and our sexual intimacy.

For many years, I was a daily drinker in an attempt to reduce my anxiety and to relax. During Lifespring, we were asked to stop drinking alcoholic beverages while enrolled in the basic and advanced trainings. Giving up Scotch, my drink of choice, turned out to be an unexpected benefit of Lifespring.

However, I continued to drink beer, and occasionally wine, for another fifteen years until going through an intensive residential program to become a raw foods vegan. As I'm writing, it's almost twenty years since I last had a "drink." Because of my ease in giving it up, I don't believe I was ever addicted to alcohol.

When we completed the Lifespring Advanced Training, it was obvious to Margaret and me that we had to concentrate on problems in our marriage. The realization led us to enroll in a retreat for couples at a ski resort in Maine. As I recall, there were twelve to fourteen couples including the four facilitators. It was an intense week in which we learned about the struggles that other couples go through. The following is a copy of a letter to Margaret that reflects on an experience I had at that retreat.

Dear Margaret,

As I'm sure you recall, we attended a couples' retreat in Maine after completing the Lifespring Advanced Training. Yesterday, an incident at the retreat came to mind. I don't recall whether I ever mentioned it to you. On the last day of the retreat, a young woman approached me with a question. I believe she and her partner were in their thirties. What she said to me still hurts 33 years later. She explained that her partner was a faculty member at Brown University and she was concerned that if she married him, he might turn out to be like me. I assume she saw me as someone who lived in my head and was emotionally distant. If my interpretation is correct, she had me pegged. Margaret, I am writing to apologize for not being emotionally available to you.

I remembered too many instances that occurred when you returned from spending time with your guru in South Fallsburg. Sitting in my chair, rather than welcoming you home, I was cold and passive-aggressive toward you. Walking through our front door must have been difficult for you.

As I ponder the difference between the stories in the above paragraphs, the first has to do with "who I was" and the second with "how I behaved toward you." Although I was largely powerless over the former, I had complete control over the latter. I deeply regret that I didn't know how to love you.

I'm sorry, Margaret. Please forgive me.

Love,

Jim

About a week after I mailed the letter, I received a telephone call from Margaret acknowledging that, like me, she didn't know how to love when we married.

Getting the Love You Want Workshop

A few years after completing Lifespring, Margaret and I enrolled in a weekend workshop led by Harville Hendrix, author of *Getting the Love You Want*. Creating a conscious marriage was the emphasis of the workshop. On the second morning, we were asked to independently write out our relationship vision. As I was busy making a list, I noticed that Margaret was not writing. When we broke for lunch, Margaret was about as angry as I ever recall seeing her. In addition to not creating her own vision of our marriage, she felt that I was busy creating demands on her which was the last thing that she wanted.

After lunch, Hendrix asked for a couple to demonstrate a "containing rage" exercise. I nudged Margaret and said "let's go" and raised my hand. As we sat looking at each other on the stage, my role was to listen and Margaret's was to talk about her anger. She exploded with memories of being inhibited in her childhood. Her emotional release proved Hendrix's dictum: "Remember, you are married to a wounded person."

Unfortunately, this new insight into Margaret's unhappiness almost thirty years into our marriage did not lead to creating a vision for a conscious marriage. In retrospect, it was too late for that. As I approached retirement, it became clear that Margaret had a much different vision than I did. Had I been conscious of her childhood wounds twenty years earlier, and had been mature and secure enough to understand how I was throwing salt on her wounds rather than contributing to healing them, our marriage might have survived. But I was neither and our marriage didn't survive.

Men's Work

Attending the New England Men's retreat led by poet Robert Bly was another turning point in my life. My first experience of "men's work" led to meeting Hines Mathews, who became my closest male friend in my adult life. In many ways, men's work was a belated response to the women's liberation movement, which challenged the patriarchy I grew up in. Rather than a role reversal, this challenge to patriarchy empowered women to recognize and practice their masculine, assertive sides, and men to cultivate their kinder, gentler, feminine sides. Coming from a patriarchal family, when Margaret and I married, I had little concept of what constitutes an equitable, caring relationship.

During the early 1990s, Hines and I participated in many men's retreats and gatherings. Being with men who were searching for meaning was both safe and enlightening. After my first men's retreat, I co-founded a men's group that met on a weekly basis in Delaware. About a year later, a different weekend workshop led to my becoming part of a second men's group that met every week in Northern Virginia, a two-hour drive for me. As I look back, participating in workshops and weekly discussions with male friends in the 90s made it the best decade of my life. I was no longer concentrating on my failing marriage. This magic period ended when I experienced a second bout of clinical depression during our divorce process. As noted earlier, my first was when I became a father.

As my marriage was coming apart, I read *The Chalice and the Blade,* in which Raine Eisler concluded that relationships between men and women follow either a dominator model or a partnership model with cultural variations in between.[3] As a consequence of the women's movement in this country, a partnership model seemed to be slowly replacing the dominator model of the patriarchy, thus allowing both women and men to lead more balanced lives. Having said that, as I am writing in 2021, the dominator model remains active in many marriages and relationships. In 1994, Congress passed the Violence Against Women Act. When I lived in Massachusetts, my interest in protecting women led me to volunteer as a courthouse advocate for individuals, mostly women, who were petitioning the court to receive a "protection from abuse" restraining

3 Eisler, Raine, *The Chalice and the Blade* (New York: Harper San Francisco, 1987).

order. "Domestic violence is motivated by power and control" was drummed into us during our training. The proliferation of handguns contributes to male power and leads to relationships based on fear, which is the opposite of love.

Cancer

As I approached retirement, Margaret and I had decided to divorce and told our children about our plans to do so. A few months later, I was diagnosed with prostate cancer. As I was walking to my office one day, it hit me that I couldn't deal with going through a divorce and surviving cancer at the same time. Because the divorce had been my idea, I told Margaret that I needed to concentrate on my health. She agreed to cancel our divorce plans and to help me explore options to eliminate the cancer. Following the advice of an alternative oncologist, we went to Pittsburgh to explore cryosurgery with one of the doctors who developed the procedure. This new technique was less invasive than the radical prostatectomy, which my urologist in Delaware told me was the "gold standard" procedure. After an evaluation, I learned that I was a good candidate for cryosurgery and was told that I was likely to be impotent after it. At sixty-two, this news did not faze me. About a month later, the procedure was performed by the doctor in Pittsburgh. Margaret supported me during the procedure and the recovery process and we stayed married.

Separation and Divorce

After I retired, Margaret and I moved to a co-housing community in Asheville, North Carolina, hoping to get a fresh start in our marriage. It soon became clear, however, that we had totally different visions for my retirement years; Margaret was committed to her career, teaching Reiki healing, and spending time with her guru as she had been doing for more than a decade. Other than spending more time together in a new location, I didn't have a vision for my retirement years.

A year after moving to Asheville, we separated and Margaret moved back to Delaware to help Cathy with our new grandson. When I proposed mediation rather than pursuing a contentious legal process, Margaret agreed. Being somewhat of an idealist, I envisioned ending our marriage as friends and even proposed having my minister perform a divorce ceremony attended by our children. That never happened. At our first and only mediation session, Margaret didn't say anything. On the way back to our condo, I noted how quiet she had been, and she replied, "I can't stand up to you." That ended mediation and Margaret hired an attorney forcing me to do likewise. After forty-three years of marriage, we divorced on December 13, 2001.

The legal process drove a deeper wedge into our relationship that took many years to heal. Eventually, about ten years after our divorce, my anger toward Margaret began to recede. As I'm writing these words, the anger is completely gone and has been replaced by empathy. Almost seventeen years after our divorce, I received these lines in an email from Margaret: "Until I took my freedom, I did not have a clue about who I was, and I am still learning. Thank you for being patient with me and agreeing to [let me] go free." Looking back, I did not know who I was either. Our divorce was the beginning of new, richer lives for both of us.

The Good Times

The good times in our marriage tended to be related to travel and time spent as a family. With my summers free, we camped for eleven years, including one trip across the United States by way of Texas, and a second trip across Canada. As the children got older, these were rare times when we had the family together. Margaret and I made several enjoyable trips to visit her relatives in Scotland and London. On our second trip, we took our children with us. Several years later, Margaret and I lived in England for four months while I conducted research on the impact of the emerging European Union on United States corporations.

During the 1980s, I taught in London five times during the university winter session. I also taught in Bulgaria twice during the nineties. Margaret went with me on these assignments. These were good times for me, but not necessarily for Margaret because she was the "tag-along" mate who supported me in my work. Increasingly, Margaret preferred to be at her guru's ashram in New York state or in India. After our decade of family camping trips in the seventies, in 1980, we bought a cottage in Maine, where I spent my summers. But I was frequently there alone while Margaret was at her ashram as we increasingly led separate and parallel lives. By this time, our children were grown. At some point, I found it easier to be alone at the cottage rather than having Margaret there with me during the infrequent times she showed up.

What It Was Like Being Married to Me

Sixty-one years after our marriage and almost twenty years after our divorce, I received a letter from Margaret. The letter begins with: *"I say all this to release my karma with you.*

Now it's up to you to release your own karma. Do as you will. All I ask is empathy from you." The letter went on to point out the many things she did to support me in my career. When we married in our twenties, after dating for a year and a half, we hardly knew each other. More importantly, we didn't know ourselves. We had never heard the term 'childhood wound', and therefore, had no idea how wounded we were. We had no concept of how poorly we were prepared for marriage. I was emotionally unavailable and afraid of my sexuality. I had no concept of how self-absorbed I was and how fragile my mental health was.

In her letter, Margaret wrote, *"I took care of you through all your depressions. The one with the birth of Carol, our first child, was most difficult."* After reading the letter, I realized that I lacked gratitude—appreciation consciousness, terms that I had little or no awareness of during our marriage. Even worse, until I read and digested her letter, I had blamed Margaret for the problems in our marriage, as well as during and after our divorce.

My attitude changed when I received that letter from Margaret asking for empathy. Quoting Margaret's letter, *"I am going to remind you of some of the things in life you may have taken for granted—all the help I have given you."* She went on to list ten points. Here is one example: *"I took care of our [four] children growing up and I cooked and cleaned our house so you could relax at home after a long day at work."* In retrospect, having grown up in a patriarchal setup, I did, in fact, take Margaret's contributions to our marriage for granted.

My first reaction to her letter was to nitpick some of the items on her list and to defend myself. But as I reread her letter, which was written as she was dealing with cancer, something changed in me; appreciation and compassion for Margaret emerged. I felt love for her for the first time since our contentious divorce almost two decades earlier. I regret that as Margaret approached her last days, she was harboring resentment toward me for events in our marriage, some of which happened more than fifty years ago.

Reading her letter, I learned to look at myself honestly and to take responsibility for my "stuff." Of equal or more importance, I learned the significance of recognizing Margaret's potential early in our marriage and how I might have encouraged her to achieve it. Had I known this, would Margaret and I still be married and have lived happily ever after? Probably not. We would have flowed with the ups and downs of life and likely would have gone our separate ways when I retired because we had different visions for the rest of our lives. However, I believe we would have parted as friends.

What was it like being married to me? I now realize how hard it was for Margaret. A major reason is that I was self-absorbed and lacked empathy. Having said that, I've been pondering the meaning of three events mentioned previously that occurred during our marriage:

1. After meeting Margaret, one of my therapists said: "Margaret feels like a bird in a cage and you are her jailer."

2. When I asked Margaret why she was quiet during a divorce mediation session, she said, "I can't stand up to you."

3. Sometime after our divorce, Margaret wrote to me, "Until I took my freedom from you, I didn't know who I was."

I believe these events say more about Margaret than they do about me. She grew up in a Scottish patriarchal family, where her father favored her two brothers. To some extent, I believe she projected anger toward her father onto me. I imagine a similar dynamic plays out in many marriages.

This background may help you to understand my frame of reference and motivation for writing this book. In short, I knew little about love when we married. In this book, I'm sharing what I have learned during my eighties. Better late than never. I have written to Margaret and we have talked out our differences. Now, I hope and pray that she will die in peace. In this context, I wrote this letter to Margaret.

October 26, 2020

Dear Margaret,

This morning, during a guided meditative program to understand and move beyond my anxiety, I realized that losing control is my greatest fear. As a child living over the funeral home, I was programmed to control my spontaneity and my emotions. I can remember Martha telling me, "Jimmie, there's a funeral on, you've got to be quiet." My fear of losing control played out in our marriage in two ways. First, to control my environment, I had to attempt to control you and the children. As you know, Jeff was a challenge in this regard. Second, my anxiety played out in our sex life with something uncontrollable—premature ejaculations. I was not able to "let go" and allow nature to run its course. I deeply regret that I didn't know what was causing my sexual dysfunction. I know it was frustrating and difficult for you.

Do you recall Cliff Smith, one of my therapists, saying, "Margaret feels like a bird in a cage and you are her jailer?" I wish I could have understood that wisdom and changed my behavior to encourage your freedom to be you rather than inhibiting it as I did.

I'm sorry, Margaret.

Love,

Jim

About a week later, I received this message from Margaret on my answering machine: "You are always forgiven and please forgive me for I tried to control you with fear and anger."

It's been years since I've seen Margaret. She lives in Honolulu, in hospice care, and her days are numbered. It feels good for both of us to let go of past hurts and reconnect in the time we have available to talk to each other. Our divorce has been good for both of us; it opened the way for each of us to follow our individual paths toward the goal of enlightenment. From reports of people who have seen her following a stroke that let her bedridden, Margaret is at peace and is an inspiration to others. I believe that her decades of meditation have allowed her to achieve "self-realization," which means that she will no longer be required to be reincarnated (a belief she holds) to complete her spiritual work on the earth plane. This has been Margaret's goal since she began following the Hindu path.

Conclusion

As a young child, I was programmed to control myself and become someone other than the real me. The same thing happened in my marriage. Margaret wanted me to be someone other than who I was. In fairness to her, I also wanted her to be someone other than who she was. My lack of acceptance repeated the pattern of her father, who squelched her dream when he told her, "women are not doctors". This dynamic led to a marriage that was stressful for both of us. Neither of us felt accepted by our partner. I take responsibility for my part in failing to encourage my wife to develop a life of her own. My assumption that like our parents, we would have a patriarchal marriage changed when women's liberation pulled the rug out from under my feet. Unfortunately, I was slow in accepting and adjusting to this cultural "sea change."

When I married at twenty-four, if I had known what I know now, I believe we could have created a good marriage. However, through all the many ups and downs, we stayed together for forty-three years. No one has had a greater influence on who I have become than Margaret. If we had not had that blind date, I might be an eighty-seven-year-old bachelor today rather the father of four children and two grandchildren, all of whom I cherish. As noted earlier, I'm blessed to have good relationships with my four children today. I treasure this Father's Day message from Cathy. "Thank you very much for always being there, Dad."

Postscript

On August 30, 2020, I came home to a telephone message from Margaret wishing me a happy anniversary. I had completely forgotten the date on which we got married sixty-two years earlier. Rather than calling Margaret back, I wrote her this letter:

August 31, 2020

Dear Margaret,

Thanks for your call yesterday. Wow! Sixty-two years ago. At 86, you and I were married for half of my life. Every life has a number of life-changing events. You were part of most of mine:

Our blind date

Getting married

Becoming a father

Getting divorced

I'm reading a book, Blueprint: How DNA Makes Us Who We Are, *in which I am learning that anxiety and depression can be inherited in our gene pool. In other words, I may have been predisposed to have a nervous breakdown when Carol was born. Had we waited to have children, I believe I could have handled it better. But we lacked the wisdom to do so. Such is life. The Pennsylvania Dutch people have a saying: "Why is it we get so soon old and so late smart."*

Other than what I put you through when Carol was born, I have no regrets, Margaret. Compared to many, we had a good marriage. You were there for me when I needed you. In many ways, you made me who I am today.

Thank you, Margaret.

I Love You,

Jim

About a week later, I read the following in *The Course of Love*, a novel by Alain de Botton. "Marriage: a hopeful, generous, infinitely kind gamble taken by two people who don't know yet who they are or who the other might be, binding themselves to a future they cannot conceive of and have carefully omitted to investigate."[4] The last phrase in the quotation describes my marriage to Margaret. In our mid-twenties, we saw marriage as an end in itself, not as a means to a future we could plan together.

Pause and Ponder: *Based upon your life experiences, can you relate to de Botton's description of marriage?*

---

4 de Botton, Alain, *The Course of Love* (New York Simon and Schuster: 2016), p. 45.

Chapter 3:

My New England Decade:
Healing, Growth, and Discovery of My Muses

Preface

Something Margaret wrote to me caused me to look at the decade between our divorce and entering into the new relationship that will be discussed in Chapter 4. As noted in the last chapter, Margaret told me, "Until I gained my freedom, I didn't know who I was." In my case, until we divorced, I didn't *like* who I was during the last years of our marriage. I tried to control Margaret's behavior by being passive-aggressive. I don't recall using words of love, acceptance, praise, approval or encouragement. I was in a lot of pain and know it was painful for Margaret to be around me. I felt free when I walked out of the courthouse a divorced, single man. This began a period of growth and change for me. Developing my muses was part of that period. In ancient Greek mythology, the muses are the inspirational goddesses of literature, science, and the arts. Today, the word 'muse' can refer to anything which inspires an artist, musician, or writer.

Becoming Nana

On September 11, 2001, I was at my daughter Cindy's home in Maine. I was returning to Asheville from our Maine cottage and stopped to spend a few days with Cindy and my new granddaughter, Anya. Not having access to a television set because Cindy chooses not to have one, I was among the few people who did not see the Twin Towers fall in New York City. Anya, who will soon turn twenty, was two and a half months old on 9/11. After I got home to Asheville, I received a letter from Cindy with a picture of me asleep while sitting on a futon, with Anya sleeping on my shoulder accompanied by the message: "Anya misses your shoulder." As our divorce was being finalized, I looked at that picture and questioned why I was living alone in a three-story, four-bedroom condominium. This question caused me to make another major life decision. After our divorce was finalized, I found a renter for my condo in Asheville and moved to a condominium I purchased near Cindy's home in the Portland area. With a summer cottage overlooking the mountains of Acadia National Park for twenty-five years, I felt a heart connection to Maine.

That move opened a new chapter in my life—helping my daughter take care of Anya, who at eight months was still *real*—had not been conditioned to conform to the standards of society. Experiencing the spontaneous love of an infant is high among the blessings of life. Anya and I formed a connection that I never had with my four children. When Anya started talking, she dubbed me Nana. That remains her name for me nineteen years later.

Maine College of Art

After moving to Maine, Cindy surprised me with a Christmas gift of everything I would need to paint in oil— paints, brushes, a pallet to mix paints, and several canvases. As I result, I enrolled in evening classes at the Maine College of Art and a long-buried muse awoke. I learned about primary colors and color theory. Having little aptitude for drawing, I painted landscape scenes with mostly flowing lines. Although I went on field trips to create plein air (outdoor) paintings with my classmates, none of these were "keepers" for me. However, in our study, we have three framed studio paintings I made from photographs. And in our kitchen, we have a small painting on a piece of wood of the view from our Maine cottage that I had painted from memory. About a year ago, Mary Anne had it professionally framed as a birthday present. In doing so, she acknowledged my muse.

Chaplaincy Program

After a Sunday service at the Swedenborgian Church, which I attended for a while in Portland, I picked up an invitation to enroll in a two-year program to become an interfaith chaplain that was offered by the Chaplaincy Institute of Maine (CHIME). I joined this new program with six or seven other students and enjoyed a stimulating first year of the two-year program. But I did not continue with the second year, which emphasized the practice of being a chaplain (counseling, conducting weddings) and an internship. I realized that I didn't really want to pursue a second career as a chaplain.

In addition to studying religions of the world, the first year of the program involved many opportunities for self-discovery. One week, a shaman led us on a journey to find our totem animal. After a period of deep meditation, a squirrel scampered across my subconscious. A week or two later, we learned the practice of proprioceptive writing, a method of exploring the subconscious mind through writing. After these experiences, I started to wake up in the middle of the night with awareness of long buried memories from my past. Initially, I fought these experiences because I wanted to go back to sleep. When that didn't work, I decided to take notes on what was bubbling up from my subconscious. This experience led me to writing my memoir, parts of which are included in Chapter 1 of this book. I now realize that my writing muse had emerged during the CHIME program. In writing this book, it's obvious that my subconscious works on the manuscript while I sleep. During the night, I sometimes get up to write down insights so I won't forget them.

Meeting Eighty Women

During the CHIME program, Michael Dwinell, a former Episcopal priest, told the class, "If you can't grieve, you can't do this work." Not being able to cry, this statement made a strong impression on me. This former priest was currently working as a therapist, and I made an appointment to talk to him. After hearing my history (which included an affair with a woman in Asheville during my separation), Michael advised me to remain celibate for a year, which I did. When the year was over, I signed up with a local dating service in Portland, where I paid a fee to review the resumes of female members. If a promising match emerged, the dating service arranged the introduction. Although I may have met forty women during this process, none of them turned into a relationship.

When this led nowhere, I enrolled in several online dating services. In one case, I met a woman who lived across the parking lot in my condo development. At the other extreme, I traveled to New Hampshire to have dinner with a woman who lived in Vermont. I also met a woman in Maine, who lived two hours away. We arranged to meet in a city that was between our homes. After walking around a college campus, we had lunch.

A few days later, I received a copy of an email she had sent to a friend stating something to the effect, "I met a good man, but he never laughs." She soon followed up with an email saying she was embarrassed by her mistake; she had not intended to send me the copy. On the other hand, she said she was relieved to have communicated her reaction to our meeting. I should note that she laughed a lot.

After meeting another forty women through online dating sites without success, I abandoned my search but still retained my membership in GreenSingles.com. Living alone, receiving daily emails from women had become addictive. From reading their profiles, I learned what women in my age bracket were looking for; it had little to do with romance. Clearly, they wanted a mature relationship between equals.

Buddhism 101

In Chapter 2, you read about my experience of my wife's seeming addiction to a Hindu guru that was playing havoc with our marriage. I resented the time she was spending with her guru, which included a number of trips to India. In an attempt to reenergize the marriage, I made a trip to India with her. Although I found the trip interesting, I never bought into the *guru principle*, the teaching that one needs to be devoted to the guru in order to achieve self-realization—a term akin to enlightenment.

While living in Maine, I made several trips to the Kripalu Center for Yoga and Health in Western Massachusetts. During one trip, I enrolled in a weekend retreat led by Dr. Robert Thurman, an eminent Tibetan Scholar and associate of the Dalai Lama. Dr. Thurman teaches at Columbia University. I left the retreat with a new understanding of Buddhism and a desire to learn more about it.

During my next five years in New England, I attended classes at the Barre Center for Buddhist Studies and retreats at the Insight Meditation Society, both in central Massachusetts. Quite unlike the Tibetan Buddhism of the Dalai Lama, I came to identify with a secular approach that sees Buddhism as a path for pursuing a life without suffering. I see Secular Buddhism, which will be discussed more fully in Chapter 5, as a philosophy of life which includes understanding oneself, the domain of psychology. Having no dogma, it is not a religion.

The following is from my notes of the retreat with Robert Thurman, "The root of my suffering is identifying with my 'Jimness' and believing in an absolute boundary between myself and others. However, Jim only exists as a relational being, not as an absolute self." Thurman continued, "Everyone goes around believing 'I am the one.' But no one agrees with my belief. As a result, my universe is shattered when I find out that I am not the one. Thus, I suffer."

Living with an Artist

After backing off from online dating, one day I received an email from Muriel, a woman in the Boston area, responding to my listing on Greensingles.com. On my way to a weekend retreat at Kripalu, I stopped to meet her and we agreed to meet again. To make a long story short, after my granddaughter started school and Cindy no longer needed my help in taking care of her, Muriel sold her condo in Brookline, Massachusetts, and bought one in Amesbury, Massachusetts. The large condo was in a converted factory building across the street from another factory that had been converted into artist studios. By this point in our relationship, Muriel and I had decided to live together. I rented my condo in Maine and moved into her new condo. As an artist, Muriel painted in acrylic and created installations, a new form of artistic expression to me. I also rented a studio across the street, which I used as my man cave. As I look back, I grew as an artist during our four years together. I learned to understand and appreciate contemporary art, and even created a piece for an exhibit in our studio building. I bought a red bra, yellow panties, and blue tights and mounted them on a canvas with the outline of the shape of a woman drawn on it. Upon seeing it, another artist proclaimed: "Jim Krum did this?" I was thrilled! Then someone stole the bra, and I retired the piece that I had titled "Primary Colors." While living in Amesbury, I bought a new camera and studied with a local photographer. Each year, a group of local artists created installations at a local state park for a week. I joined Muriel in signing up to participate, and for two years, I hung my photographs on limbs of trees for the public to view.

During our first year living together, Muriel and I attended Unity on the River, a church in Amesbury Massachusetts. I enjoyed the spirited services which featured jazz musicians and also the positive talks by the minister whom I related to with ease. However, I torpedoed the experience when my dogmatic beliefs about the meaning of the word 'God' surfaced in a membership class. During the class, I challenged the minister on her use of the 'God' word, and the next Sunday, she used the authority of the pulpit to set me straight. Muriel and I were sitting in the front row and I believe she was talking directly to (or at) me. I became angry and never returned to the church. Many years later, I'm regretting that decision. Memories of these events arose recently as I was watching a YouTube recording of an old Unity on the River service with my new partner (who is a retired Unity minister). As I reflect on this life-changing experience, my arrogance and dogmatism cut me off from a meaningful part of my life living in this new community. In Chapter 5, the potentially destructive role of the egoic mind will be explored. I believe my extreme reaction can be traced to my rebellion against growing up in the Lutheran church. As I look back, I wish I had made an appointment with the minister to discuss our differences. Arrogance and anger are a destructive combination.

After my abrupt departure from Unity on the River, Muriel and I attended the Greater Boston Church of Spiritualism, where Muriel was enrolled in a mediumship course to unfold her natural ability to communicate with departed spirits. My skepticism diminished when I had a mediumship session with a young woman who seemed clearly in touch with my father's spirit. She communicated this message from him: "I'm in school. If I had known what I know now, I would have been a better father. Please pray for me." Both clues to his identity that the medium related and the message seemed authentic. In the world of mysticism, anything is possible.

After a few years living and traveling together, patterns from my marriage began to emerge, and I realized that I was living Muriel's life, not mine. Over time, my ardor cooled and our mutual acceptance of each other diminished. I recognized that this was not the relationship I wanted for the rest of my life and it was time to move on. But the question was: Where to go? More on that in the next section. Overall, Muriel and I had a good four years together. But neither of us knew how to love.

My Move to a Retirement Community

By the time I was ready to leave Muriel, Cindy and her family had moved to Honolulu, where her husband got a job and where Margaret lived. Had Cindy's family remained in Maine, I would have returned to live in my condo there. When my sister moved to a retirement community, I had my answer to the question of where to go next. I decided to move to Kendal at Longwood, a Quaker community not far from the home of my daughter, Cathy, in Delaware. This was the end of my four-teen-year post-retirement odyssey that began when Margaret and I moved to Asheville in 1998. I was back on my home turf and promptly enrolled in the Osher Lifelong Learning Institute at the University of Delaware. It was there that I met Mary Anne three years later, when she enrolled in a class I was teaching.

From the beginning, I felt like a misfit at Kendal. Having grown up living among the dead, I was now living among the dying. The move did not go as smoothly as I had hoped. Before my moving van arrived, I experienced a bout of clinical depression (the third in my life), which I blame on a Kendal psychiatrist who insisted on changing my anti-depressant medication. Regretfully, I followed his advice and crashed during the period of going off one medication and starting the new one.

A friend at Kendal had a Vizsla, a Hungarian hunting dog. Knowing the challenge I was facing in adapting to my new home, he told me about a rescue dog that was available for adoption in Philadelphia. I met Kelly and adopted her. No longer living alone, my depression gradually lifted. Kelly was a godsend to me.

Feeling totally out of my element and with women greatly outnumbering men at Kendal, I soon latched onto Martha, a woman four years older than me. This relationship outlived my decision to leave Kendal after two years. Besides wanting to regain my freedom from the institutional rules and regulations, I realized that staying at Kendal would decimate my estate. The entrance and high monthly fees reduced my estate by more than $100,000 during my two years at Kendal. When Mary Anne came into my life, my relationship with Martha ended. I regret that she felt abandoned.

Most people at Kendal seemed quite happy there and I made a number of good friends. Five of us formed a Buddhist meditation and study group. On Sunday mornings, I attended a Quaker meeting, a new experience for me. Other than feeling like a misfit there and regretting the poor financial decision I made, Kendal was a good transition to the next phase of my life.

Chapter 4:
Finding Love at Eighty

When I left Kendal, Kelly and I moved to a third-floor apartment in a farmhouse owned by a Kendal neighbor. We stayed there for two years while I continued to take and teach classes at Osher Lifelong Learning.

Although I didn't know it at the time, my life was about to change. It was the beginning of a new semester at Osher, where I taught a class called "Of Minds and Men." To facilitate discussion, I limited enrollment to fourteen students. When I entered the classroom, I saw a number of familiar faces and a few new ones. One of the new students was Mary Anne Multer. She had long, white, flowing hair that was pulled back and secured in a barrette. After a few classes, I decided to get to know her, and in her words, periodically would "show up at my elbow" in the lobby. But being overwhelmed with many new faces, she didn't immediately connect me to the class. Eventually, we did sit in a common room to talk over coffee, and according to Mary Anne, I told her my life story. Sometime later, Mary Anne reflected on her reaction: "Why is he telling me all this?" With years of psychotherapy, I guess I'm pretty much an open book.

Eventually, over the lunch table and walks at Longwood Gardens, Mary Anne's story emerged. She married before finishing college. She has three children and three grandchildren. After her marriage ended in divorce, she pursued numerous interests including teaching horseback riding and studying to become a Unity minister. After serving three congregations, Mary Anne retired and fulfilled a longtime dream by taking off in Odyssey, her twenty-two-foot Winnebago Warrior motor home, to see the country. Following twelve rewarding years on the road, for two years Mary Anne lived in an intentional community in southwest Virginia before moving to Pennsylvania to be close to one of her daughters. As she was getting acquainted with the area, she came across a schedule of Osher courses and enrolled. During her second year there, she enrolled in my course.

In addition to getting together for lunch and walks, much of our "courting" was done by email. At some point, I began signing my emails LLL (Let's Learn Love) and then LLLL (Let's Learn to Live Love). With these "Ls," the seeds of this book were planted and Mary Anne and I developed "Learning to Love" as a class that we co-taught at Osher. While I brought my scholarly background to the class, Mary Anne brought her human warmth. After teaching the class twice, I decided to turn my research and handouts into the first iteration of Chapter 5 of this book. Two years after we met, we decided to share an apartment, and after an extensive search, we found the large apartment where we now live. Mary Anne continued to attend my "Of Minds and Men" class and blushed the day I told the class that we were sharing an apartment.

After more than four years together, I realize that this is the first time in my adult life that I feel loved. Using author Martin Buber's term, Mary Anne and I are creating an "I-Thou" relationship (as opposed to an "I-It" relationship governed by the individual egos). Having a common purpose is important to the success of our relationship. Being in our eighties, we are committed to supporting each other in our remaining years. Using a metaphor, we are in a canoe paddling together to achieve the goal of richer, fuller lives. Putting our emphasis on *learning to love* has been important. Love is no longer an abstract concept. We accept and honor each other without being critical, and as a result, we both feel safe in the relationship. We are both beginning to feel lovable and to love ourselves. Our three-bedroom apartment gives us room to be alone when we want to. In addition to having our own bedrooms, we share a study. I'm a very different person than the immature man who married Margaret sixty-two years ago. My relationship with Mary Anne has blossomed and I am experiencing the best years of my life. At eighty-seven, I am blessed with good health and a relationship I never dreamed I might have.

Kelly's Last Gift

At fifteen, Kelly had been slowing down for more than a year. She spent most of her time sleeping and could (or would) no longer go on walks longer than ten minutes. Toward the end, she was experiencing trouble getting up on the sofa where she often napped. Eventually she had a problem standing up using her back legs. Kelly remained a voracious eater until one morning when she collapsed in the kitchen next to her food bowl and was not interested in eating. She took a few bits of kibble from my hand. Thus began a three-hour period during which Kelly and I communicated heart-to-heart.

Being clear that Kelly was ready to leave her body behind and approach the Rainbow Bridge of Norse folklore, I called my daughter, Cathy, who gave me the name of a husband-and-wife team of veterinarians who make house calls. When the vets returned my call, we scheduled time to take Kelly out of her misery. While waiting for them to arrive, Mary Anne and I sat silently with Kelly. Because of the coronavirus pandemic restrictions, we carried Kelly outside our front door when the vets arrived. Some of the most difficult moments of my life followed as the vets did their work. Kelly resisted until the vet gave her a shot to calm her, which was followed by a shot to end her life. I cried as Kelly's life faded and she was carried away to the vet's car on her way to be cremated. My tears were Kelly's last gift to me. I cried again when I read aloud the story of the Rainbow Bridge that Mary Anne had printed out, and later, when I read it to my children during a conference call to mourn Kelly's passing.

I reflected on how putting my dog, Cleo, down at a vet's office ten years earlier had been a totally different experience. I was completely detached from my feelings and couldn't wait to leave after the procedure. Losing Kelly proved that my heart had begun to open. I attribute much of this to Kelly who entered my life during a difficult period of clinical depression. Unlike two other dogs I have had, Kelly was an amazing presence in my life and in Mary Anne's life as well. We still think of her every day. Kelly had adapted to each of us differently. For many years Kelly had been at my feet while I cooked. However, concerned that she might trip over Kelly, Mary Anne taught her to stay out of the kitchen when she was cooking. Kelly waited patiently until Mary Anne called me for dinner. When I walked into the kitchen, Kelly jumped off the sofa and followed me.

A few hours after the vets took Kelly away, I talked to my daughter Carol who asked me how I was feeling. I replied that I was feeling sad, guilty for taking Kelly's life, and relieved that she was out of her misery. Being able to answer the *feeling* question was another breakthrough. Kelly was among the many blessings in my life.

Other Reflections on My Life[5]

We humans are conditioned (wounded) by both our childhood experiences and possibly also by our experiences in previous relationships. I was married to the same woman for half of my life. Margaret and I both carry wounds from our childhoods and from our marriage.

Pause and Ponder: *Can you relate to having people in your life who want you to be someone different than you are?*

That was my experience in my marriage to Margaret. I also wanted her to be someone different than she was. Acceptance explains why my current relationship with Mary Anne works so well. I am blessed that Mary Anne accepts living with a writer. She knows that writing my story gives meaning to my life.

Shopping for a Car

In doing the research for this book, I've learned that our psychic wounds are stored in our bodies as emotions that may erupt when stimulated. The following story describes a major eruption of my volcano, set off by an innocent telephone call that Mary Anne made to a relative. Fortunately, the lava did not spew anger because I was able to verbalize what I was experiencing in my subconscious.

The story begins when Mary Anne's daughter, who manages her investment portfolio, told her that she has plenty of money if she wanted to replace her 2004 Saturn Vue that needed repairs. This stimulated my passion for car shopping. As we looked for cars, I learned that Mary Anne has trouble spending

---

5 This section contains random reflections on my life that did not fit in elsewhere.

money on herself and has a hard time making decisions. Using her term, she "vacillates." I'm almost the polar opposite. After doing my research, I tend to be decisive but sometimes experience cognitive dissonance and question my decisions after the fact.

Our first two visits to dealership used car lots resulted in Mary Anne learning what she didn't want in terms of features and colors. After placing a deposit on one car, she changed her mind and canceled the order. Sometime later, the issue arose again when her daughter gave her a year-end report on her portfolio that prompted Mary Anne to suggest that we look at cars again. By now, I was an expert on *Consumer Reports* evaluations of late model used cars. I had also gone online to look at the used car inventories of Toyota, Honda, and Subaru dealerships. By then, I had learned that what Mary Anne wanted was (1) another SUV, (2) a Toyota, and (3) ideally, a hybrid. When I learned that Toyota makes a hybrid SUV and found a late model used one at a dealership, I made an appointment to see it. Before going to look at the vehicle, Mary Anne said she wanted to talk to a relative who had managed automobile repair shops. After talking to him, Mary Anne canceled our trip to see the Toyota. I felt like a concrete block had dropped on my chest. I was deeply hurt; and physical pain surfaced in my upper body. My mood hit the floor. I was devastated.

When I went to bed, I couldn't sleep. As I pondered my reaction to Mary Anne's phone call, memories that remained buried for decades surfaced. I thought about an incident in eighth grade when I applied to join the Junior High Y, a Y.M.C.A. program, and was rejected when I began to cry while standing on a stage in a dark room before the members. If this was supposed to be my rite of passage into manhood, I failed it. Until putting two dogs down within the last ten years, this may have been the last time I cried. Then an event during the *est* training some forty years ago popped up in my mind. I recalled being on a stage with a group of other men when the trainer asked me, "Where are your balls, man?" I felt humiliated when I left the stage. Lastly, the sexual incompatibility in my marriage came to mind. Because a man is expected to *perform,* I assumed the problem was because of my inadequacy.

I now recognize that my interest in and knowledge of cars is part of my masculinity. When Mary Anne took the advice of someone who knows much more about cars than I do, my male ego was bruised and my repressed anger surfaced. However, I didn't explode in rage or withdraw into myself to brood and become passive-aggressive as had been my style during my marriage. Instead, I endeavored to understand the hurts that caused my reaction. When I recovered my equanimity, I made it clear to Mary Anne that she had done nothing wrong. It was all my stuff. As we talked, I recognized that my strong reaction to an innocent telephone call had deeply hurt Mary Anne.

A Course in Miracles states: "Love brings up everything unlike itself for purposes of healing and release."[6] What is important is what we do when an event that undermines our ego occurs. The physical pain I experienced when Mary Anne called her relative was in the solar plexus, where several nerves intersect and is often associated with fear. My fight or flight reaction was activated as fear arose. Fortunately, I was able to access the middle ground between lashing out and running away. I did this by telling Mary Anne much of the above story, and especially my feelings. By sharing it, I got it off my chest.

---

6 Foundation for Inner Peace, *A Course in Miracles* (Tiburon, CA: Foundation for Inner Peace, 1975, 1985).

Pause and Ponder: *If you are a man, can you relate to my story? If you can, consider taking time to write your version of the story. Writing can bring clarity and healing. If you are a woman, have you experienced the bruised male ego? Consider writing about that.*

More than a year after the car shopping events described above, awareness of the influence of cars on global warming stimulated my desire to buy a hybrid car to replace the two aging cars Mary Anne and I own. We decided that we no longer needed two cars. A pleasant walk in a state park was ruined when I introduced the subject of buying a hybrid. Once again, my decisiveness and Mary Anne's reluctance to change butted heads. After dinner, the tightness in my chest told me that we needed to talk about our feelings. During our talk, Mary Anne told me she had written about her anger when we came home from the walk. I told her that I was feeling shitty and would probably have trouble sleeping. Talking out what we were feeling released the tension. I slept well, and in the morning, told Mary Anne that I wanted to put off further consideration about buying a car until I finished editing the manuscript of this book. She agreed. Eventually, Mary Anne and I leased a car with the latest accident-prevention features.

Hitting a Wall

On your journey of learning to give and receive love, you are likely to run into a wall at some point with *your* name on it. I call it the "*I, me, mine*" wall, the very wall that I encountered in the story about Mary Anne's car shopping. Breaking down that wall requires venturing into unknown territory, the quantum field of infinite possibilities. However, you can't enter the quantum field with a linear goal created by your rational mind. Overcoming one's egoic mind requires both the courage to change and a commitment of time and energy to explore the mystical realm, where your true loving nature resides. Be patient. Buddhist monks take decades to pursue the enlightenment that the Buddha achieved.

The *I, me, mine* wall is like an addiction to a way of reacting to protect our ego. This raises the question of whether we are the masters of our minds or their servants. As humans, we must first be aware of our tendency to react without thinking. Both Buddhism and Science of Mind come down on the side of mastering the mind. Both are based on the premise that you can teach yourself to think differently, and therefore, to respond with love. These two philosophies for achieving a more enlightened state of consciousness are discussed in Chapter 5.

To get there requires gaining insights into the subconscious mind, which drives much of our behavior. Rather than being powerless over our egoic mind, each of us has the ability to break through our unique wall because our brain is flexible and can be changed. This, of course, requires work to reprogram the brain. Buddhist scholar Robert Thurman believes that even children can be educated to break out of the prison of self-concern. In other words, they can learn to love.

Tipping Points

As I look back at my life, I am aware of tipping points where the trajectory of my life changed dramatically. These meaningful coincidences had a big impact on my life. In working with patients, Swiss psychiatrist and psychoanalyst Carl Jung identified synchronicities in their lives. Mary Anne refers to them as "divine order." However, our future is not solely determined by the synchronicities that present us with opportunities to change. How we respond to these coincidences is always our choice. Three examples from my life follow.

As related earlier, during the second semester of my senior year in college, a chance encounter with the college placement director led to a job with Westinghouse Electric Corporation, which several months later led to a blind date with Margaret. That encounter changed my life.

While living at Kendal, one afternoon I was walking to a meeting of a men's group I helped start. On the way, I encountered a friend. Out of the blue, Ed said, "Jim, moving here is the dumbest thing I've ever done." Without thinking, I replied, "Ed, moving here is the dumbest thing I've ever done." My reaction set in motion my decision to leave. The synchronicity of this chance meeting also altered the direction of my life.

The third was Mary Anne's enrollment in my class. In addition to bringing love into my life, as a retired Unity minister, Mary Anne introduced me to New Thought spirituality, which complements the insights of the Buddha to form the philosophical underpinnings of this book.

My Eighty-Seven Year Journey

During our journey through life, we each face a number of choices. As I reflect on my life, the following were major turning points:

- Leaving the funeral home to go to college.
- Marrying Margaret.
- Having four children.
- Becoming a college professor.

- Seeking marriage counseling that led to decades of individual psychotherapy and self-knowledge.
- Getting divorced.
- Leaving the Christian tradition and eventually finding the secular Buddhist path.
- After meeting Mary Anne, deciding it was time to *learn to love*.
- Writing this book.

Pause and Ponder: *What were the turning points that changed the trajectory of your life?*

As noted earlier, walking out of a concert hall one night, I turned to Mary Anne and said: "I've had a good life. I'm having a good life. I'm going to continue having a good life." This realization does not mean that my life has been easy or devoid of suffering. I still live with chronic anxiety. In retrospect, I have navigated the challenges of life well, and at eighty-seven, I am experiencing the best years of my life.

While reading my manuscript, my friend Steve Johnson posed this question. "Jim, you have mentioned other relationships with women. When love is new, everything is rosy. You are pulled out of compulsive loneliness. After a time, old patterns reemerge. What is different now? Perhaps your answer will be, "I learned to love." You are right, Steve. To the best of my ability, I'm practicing what I'm "preaching" in this book, and it works. I'm blessed to have a partner who is a pleasure to live with. Mary Anne and I are creating what Martin Buber termed an "I-Thou" relationship.

Chapter 5:

A Roadmap for Creating Love in *Your* Life

Preface

You have just read highlights of the first eighty-seven years of my life's story. I've learned a lot pulling it together to write this book. Now it's time for you to contemplate *your* unique life story. This part of the book is interactive. It presents various elements in the framework I have developed to understand my life. In Chapter 5, you will encounter opportunities to stop and contemplate your life. Take time to *pause and ponder* when prompted to do so. Keeping a *learning to love* journal is a good way to compile your insights.

Learning to love is comparable to putting a puzzle together. There are many interconnecting pieces, which are discussed in the following sections. You will find *pieces of the puzzle* at the end of most sections. Because this will be an *active* process, I have divided Chapter 5 into three acts. "Understanding Yourself I: Being Human," the theme of Act 1, begins with a discussion of levels of consciousness that is followed by an overview of the teachings of the Buddha and New Thought spirituality. It concludes with a discussion of the distinction between "nature and nurture."

Act 2 explores understanding our "Barriers to Love" and is based on this wisdom of Jalal Rumi, a 13th century Persian poet, Islamic scholar, and Sufi mystic: "Your task is not to seek for love, but merely to seek and find the barriers within yourself that you have built up against it."[7] The colloquial term "stuff" will sometimes be used in discussing an individual's barriers to love. Self-examination and discovery require a willingness to be vulnerable and to drop one's facade or outward appearance.

We must understand our unique barriers to love before we can remove them and change our lives. Two books, *The Second Mountain: The Quest for a Moral Life by* David Brooks and *Living with the Devil: A Meditation on Good and Evil* by Buddhist scholar, Stephen Batchelor are discussed in Act 2. The twelve-step recovery program, Co-Dependents Anonymous, also provided inspiration for Act 2.

Act 3, "The Practice of Love," follows Viktor Frankl's advice: "Love is the only way to grasp another human being in the innermost core of his personality. No one can become fully aware of the very essence of another human being unless he loves him. By his love, he is enabled to see the essential traits and features in the beloved person; and even more, he sees that which is potential in him, which is not yet actualized but yet ought to be actualized. Furthermore, by his love, the loving person enables the beloved person to actualize these potentialities."[8] After surviving life in two German concentration camps, the Austrian neurologist and psychiatrist wrote *Man's Search for Meaning.* In contrast to Rumi, Frankl's perspective of love emphasizes encouraging the beloved in the same way that enlightened parents encourage each of their children to achieve their unique potentials. The Rumi and Frankl perspectives on love complement each other.

---

7 Rumi, Jalal (1207-1273) *Rumi Quotations* (Goodreads.com).

8 Frankl, Viktor, *Man's Search for Meaning* (New York: Pocket Books, 1963) pp. 176-7.

The book compiles what I have learned about love from both scholarly research and personal experience in my new relationship with Mary Anne. The material tends to be *prescriptive* as well as *descriptive*. Because each of us is unique, some may find it difficult to relate to some of it. However, be cautious about dismissing the concepts you will encounter in this chapter as irrelevant. Many years ago, I had a t-shirt that said, "Denial is not a river in Egypt."

Act 1. Understanding Yourself: Being Human
Preface: How Conscious Are You?

As you begin to read Act 1, please contemplate these questions:

- Do you desire to have a loving relationship in your life?
- Do you want to change?
- Are you *willing* to change?

If you answered the three questions in the affirmative, do you *intend* to change?

If you intend to change, do you know *how* to change? If you don't know how to change, you're in good company.

Are you ready to embrace introspection to raise your consciousness?

Before proceeding, we must look at another critical question: Are you *willing* to encourage your partner to grow and change?

In creating a loving relationship, encouraging your partner to grow and change requires *love intelligence*. We will begin by looking at what it means to live *consciously*, which includes developing our *love consciousness*. The opposite, of course, is living *unconsciously*. In addition to human psychology, we delve into the realm of metaphysics to define consciousness. If one is conscious, one is aware of his/her *internal states*, which include thoughts and feelings, and also is aware of *external events*. If you can verbalize something you are experiencing, then it is part of your consciousness. Exploring dysfunctional patterns in our subconscious is also important because much of our behavior is guided by our automatic reactions that are guided by our emotions. Learning to love may require breaking these patterns.

Before proceeding, we need to pause and define the meaning of *mind*, a common word that lacks a clear definition because the mind is not an organ like the brain that can be observed using scans. Clearly, the conscious and unconscious mind is the repository of memories. However, the mind is not limited to memories of experiences that are stored in the brain. A later section will examine memories, often painful, that are stored in the *body-mind*, which spiritual teacher and author Eckhart Tolle calls the "pain body".

The Five Mind States

In an overview of the basic principles of Science of Mind, Rev. Lloyd Strom identified five *mind states*.[9]

1. The *primal mind state* is all about the instincts of the basic human animal with little awareness of thoughts, feelings, or emotions. The primary motivations for

---

9 Strom, Rev. Lloyd, *Religious Science Quick Start*, (Novato, CA: Nova Tech 2010).

individuals experiencing a primal mind state are survival, seeking pleasure, and avoiding pain.

2.   The *reactive mind state* is ruled by emotional responses to the outside world that it attempts to control to feel safe. Events may trigger memories of the past that are buried in the body; these emotions can unconsciously preempt the rational mind. Thus, the reactive mind state is ruled by emotions, not reason.

3.   The *rational mind state* attempts to succeed through its own efforts and thus tends to be egocentric. In contrast to the reactive mind, the rational mind represses emotions. It sees the world as a series of problems to be solved, which may include learning to love. Solving this problem may lead to love intelligence but not love consciousness.

4.   The *mystical mind state* has awakened to the greater possibilities of human existence and develops an intuitive awareness of oneness with others, and with the source of all life, which is called by many names: God, universal intelligence, and one's higher power. As this sense of oneness or unity increases, the ego of the rational mind retreats into the background. "Let go and let God," a slogan of twelve-step recovery work, catches the essence of relying on the *intuition* of the mystical mind.

5.   In the *enlightened mind state,* the ego of the rational mind disappears completely as love consciousness takes over. If we look at being human as a creative process, achieving an enlightened mind is the apex, the highest level of human consciousness, in which individual humans realize their true nature.

Enlightenment is a state achieved by messiahs like the Buddha and Jesus, and by other mystics. Although realization of our true nature may not be achieved during our lifetime, enlightenment is a worthy goal to pursue.

The five mind states construct was created to describe levels or states of human consciousness. Observing behavior gives clues to how conscious an individual is in any given situation. We've all heard the statement, "He/she is so unconscious." The mind state paradigm is a tool for individuals to evaluate how conscious they are in situations like marriage. Are we conscious of our own needs? Of our partner's needs?

The *tension of the opposites* concept that will be explored in Act 3 suggests that individuals are often pulled in two different directions at the same time, e.g., the primal mind pulls in one direction while the rational mind pulls in the opposite direction. This is consistent with Freud's concept of the id (primal mind) and superego (moral standards) being moderated by the ego (the rational mind). In the case of sexual abuse and rape, the id wins because of poor ego control over the primal mind state.

Pause and Ponder: *Of the five mind states, is there one that dominates your "operating system?"*

Before studying states of consciousness, I saw myself as a rational human being who lives largely in "my head." I had no idea that feelings and emotions frozen in my body dictated maybe ninety-five percent of my reactions, and therefore, my behavior. I now recognize that past experiences inhibit my ability to experience love consciousness because my responses to events and people are largely determined by unconscious reactions. Returning to the question of which mind state runs my daily life, it's now clear to me that the reactive state does and that I must learn to become conscious of when and how it does. Learning to love requires knowing and understanding your reactive mind.

Pause and Ponder: *In your life experiences, would you describe your state of mind as being "unconscious" most of the time?*

Two words—awaken and awareness—are often used to describe the two highest levels of consciousness, the realms of love and connection—as opposed to separation.

- *Awaken* to the greater possibilities of human existence.
- *Awareness,* centered in the spiritual center of the being, which is sometimes called the *transcendental heart.*

Let's explore the meanings of these two key "A" words: *Awaken* to what? *Aware* of what? The Buddha was referred to as the "Awakened One," meaning he became *aware* of his authentic nature as a human being, the nature he was born with. Learning to love involves creating *awareness* of reactions that result from past experiences, dogma, ignorance, arrogance, and/or insistence on particular outcomes. This requires a fluid mind that does not get bogged down in contradictions, a mind that is not run by buried emotions that originated in our formative years. A goal of learning to love is to become free of these reactions stemming from the past. Achieving this freedom requires following a path that leads to *awakening* to our true nature--which is love.

The paradigm of the five mind states presents a continuum progressing from a low level of consciousness (primal) to the highest level (enlightened). The continuum goes from emphasis on selfishly fulfilling one's *primal* needs to the complete selflessness of the *enlightened* mind state. It suggests a goal of awakening one's innate love to achieve one's higher human potential. However, it's a mistake to devalue the "lowest" mind state. We were born with primal urges which serve a critical purpose in the procreation of the human species through "making love." The ability to experience appropriate spontaneous, primal energy without guilt is vital to creating a healthy sexual union between two people.

To fully comprehend how the mind works, it is necessary to understand the concepts of the unconscious (sometimes referred to as the body-mind) and the subconscious mind. These states rule the reactive mind state. The term "unconscious" is associated with Freud. Later, Jung used the term "collective unconscious" to describe how individuals have imbibed a culture. For example, I believe the collective unconscious of most European-Americans is racist based on the assumption of white privilege.

Although the rational mind may be considered the ideal in our culture, the flow of consciousness among all mind states is required in a healthy human being. While an active rational mind may be counterproductive in the act of making love, it plays an important role in freeing us from being run by the instincts of the primal mind and the habitual patterns of the reactive mind, and also in recognizing the importance of becoming aware of our true nature.

Change and growth are not linear. In the yin/yang diagram that comes from Taoism in China, this interrelationship is conveyed by a circle in which the white part symbolizes *yang* (the male assertive part), and the black represents (*yin*), the soft, feminine part of being human. The white dot in the dark (yin) part of the circle and the black dot in the light (yang) part of the circle conveys the belief that every yin has some yang in it and every yang has some yin in it. These light and dark sides of the human psyche are meant to coexist in harmony. When applied appropriately, both energies are required to be completely human. As we are learning to love, we must accept these two complementary components of our human nature and flow with them.

Examples of the Five Mind States

For clarity, we will explore dimensions and examples of the five levels of consciousness, beginning with the *primal* mind. As a man, my *primal mind* awakens to women I find attractive or sexy. Therefore, I need a moral code to keep a check on it. The primal mind of women is different. Being biologically programmed to reproduce, women have a comparable sexual urge.

Fear and anger are two buried emotions that can rule the *reactive mind* state. But how did they develop? I have traced my anxious temperament back to an event when I must have been about three. My father was listening to the radio in our living room and I was playing with my toys on the floor. At some point, I decided to put my toys away in a bronze kettle as I had been taught to do. The noise disturbed my father, who yelled at me and sent me to my room. I can remember pleading, "I was only trying to help." As I ponder the experience, I believe many children would have cried to release the hurt they felt. But I didn't cry; I believe that stuffed emotion remains in my body creating anxiety. As noted earlier, I remember waking up during the night and going to our housekeeper's bedroom and saying, "Marty, I'm scared." That fear is still "in my bones" and inhibits my love consciousness. And, as noted in the stories about my sister and about my marriage, I know that anger lurks below my conscious mind.

The *rational mind* state is ruled by the ego where life is all about *I, me, and mine.* Although the rational mind employs a cognitive thinking process, don't conclude that it is the seat of truth of the reality of a situation. The conclusions of the rational mind depend on one's reasoning skills, which vary greatly, and one's unconscious assumptions; there are likely to be alternate explanations of reality that are not considered. Of course, one's emotional state also affects rational thinking. As a child, I needed to develop my cognitive abilities to solve the problem of what was expected of me in my unusual home environment. My cognitive skills served me well in my academic career, where I conducted scholarly research and trained students to use their rational minds to solve problems.

Degree of self-control is a critical variable in identifying mind states. As noted earlier, the individual who is overtaken by his/her primal mind state has limited self-control and, therefore, is capable of brutality. However, positively, functioning in the primal mind state allows one to engage in healthy sexual intercourse. The individual whose anger is easily provoked in his/her *reactive mind* has the potential to perpetrate violence in a relationship. On the other hand, the *rational mind* is synonymous with a high level of self-control. But one must let go of that control to enter the *mystical* and *enlightened* mind states. "Accessing the Mystical Mind State" is discussed in the next section.

In addition to Science of Mind, the term "enlightenment" shows up in both the Hindu and Buddhist wisdom traditions. The following words are attributed to the Buddha:

"... with enlightenment there is no liking or disliking. All dualities come from ignorant inference ... Gain and loss, right and wrong: such thoughts must finally be abolished. To come directly into harmony with this reality, just simply say when doubt arises, 'Not two.' In this 'not two,' nothing is separate, nothing is excluded. No matter when or where, enlightenment means entering this truth."

Pause and Ponder: *Does the above statement ring true to you? If not, what parts of it do you have a problem with?*

Since first encountering the concept of duality more than thirty years ago at a Hindu ashram, I have struggled with understanding it. If duality is new to you, be patient.

The three lower mind states played out in my marriage beginning on our honeymoon as discussed in Chapter 2. Raised with Lutheran guilt, I was taught that premarital sex was a sin. But after holy matrimony was bestowed by a minister, sex was now allowed. A "Thou shalt not" was removed. But the message was not replaced by "thy shall enjoy thy sexuality." To illustrate how unaware I was growing up, about the time I reached puberty, a friend told me about sexual intercourse. I responded, "My parents would never do that." I had never even seen them hug or kiss.

In learning to love, our goal is to become conscious of our mind state at every moment in our waking life. When we are mindful, we can choose the appropriate response to any situation based upon our core values. A second and equally important goal is to become conscious of and cultivate the higher mind states that reside below our normal consciousness. This process is termed "unfoldment."

Love Consciousness

I have made a distinction between *love intelligence* and *love consciousness.* In the former, the rational mind state can learn *how* to love, but love consciousness does not reside in the head. Instead, think of *depth,* the "ground of your being," using theologian Paul Tillich's term. As humans, I believe experiencing love is part of our nature when we are born. However, if not cultivated, our loving nature gets covered up by emotions like fear and anger and by the cognitive training of our rational minds to solve problems. Therefore, to experience love consciousness, we must surrender to the realm of the mystical mind state. Meditation and contemplation are the doors to rising above our thoughts and possibly experiencing moments of enlightenment, the realm of pure love. Meister Eckhart, a thirteenth century German theologian, philosopher, and mystic said, "What a man takes in by contemplation, that he pours out in love."[10]

Love intelligence requires becoming aware that your beloved experiences the same continuum of mind states from primal to enlightened. At any given moment, your beloved may be rational, reactive, or even primal, and may be out of sync with you. Codependency occurs when one party fears the reactions of the partner and creates behavior patterns to avoid provoking negative reactions. This has been referred to as "walking on eggshells." A relationship is a dance between states

---

10 www.brainyquotes/quotes/meistereckhart.

of consciousness that are sometimes in sync and at other times at odds.

In conclusion, human beings have the potential to experience higher mind states. But achieving them is not a linear process as the paradigm of the five mind states might suggest. A starting point is recognizing that our *body-minds* (the realm of feelings and emotions) create stimuli that we react to. Thus, in learning to love, humans must *consciously* develop their rational mind state. However, accessing the mystical mind state (the door to unconditional love) requires a practice like dream interpretation, meditation, journaling, and/or prayer.

A Piece of the Puzzle

Emotional responses from the reactive mind come from past experiences, especially painful ones. Because the reactive mind state controls most of our moment-to-moment perceptions of and reactions to events, it can present a fundamental barrier to giving and receiving love. *Learning to love* requires raising your consciousness to your rational mind, a cognitive process. However, *experiencing love* ascends beyond that cognitive mind state through a mystical process.

Accessing the Mystical Mind State

As noted earlier, when I lived in Massachusetts for a number of years after my divorce, I sometimes attended the Greater Boston Church of Spiritualism, where Muriel, my partner at the time, was learning to master the process of unfoldment in order to become a spiritual medium. As I understand it, unfoldment is a process of raising consciousness to the mystical mind state.

A quantum leap from the rational to *mystical* mind state represents an abrupt transition from one discrete energy state to another. As one awakens to the greater possibilities of life in the mystical mind state, the egoic rational mind recedes into the background. In our Western culture, this shift to love consciousness is a mystery to the rational mind. It requires mindfulness, the ability to be present in the moment, the *now.* Whether that "now" is experienced as joyful or sad does not matter. Experiencing sadness is superior to repressing it.

In comparison to achieving success through the intellectual effort of one's rational mind state, the *mystical* mind state is in touch with the deeper realities of human consciousness; understanding that we all are one, not separate. Note the shift from reliance on the egoic mind to a loving heart connection, which in essence is a shift from "I" thinking to "we" thinking. Intuition, a sense of knowing without rational thinking, is the fruit of the mystical mind state. Yielding to the mystical mind state involves a "leap of faith." The slogan "let go and let God" represents this leap in twelve-step programs, where the second step is "came to believe that a power greater than myself can return me to sanity," and the third step is "made a decision to turn my will and my life over to the care of the God of my understanding." In recovering from addictions, this "higher power" of the mystical mind state replaces the primal, reactive, or rational mind states.

Intuition has been defined as the ability to understand something immediately without the need for conscious reasoning. In other words, one is incapable of creating a shift to the mystical mind state using the intellect. Instead, it requires adopting a practice of unfolding our natural intuition. For example, *insight meditation* is a Buddhist practice designed to access the mystical mind state by observing blocks to love created by lower states of human consciousness. Also, in comparison with the rational mind state, which suppresses troublesome emotions that arise, an individual with a mystical mind state has attained *freedom* from the impact of those emotions.

A Piece of the Puzzle

Love consciousness is a mystery to the rational mind. Intuition is the ability to understand something immediately without the need to try to figure it out. *Awakening* is the Buddhist term for accessing the mystical mind state.

The Buddha's Insights and New Thought Spirituality

Unity and Science of Mind, both New Thought philosophies, and the insights of the Buddha differ largely in terminology, not in substance. Both are concerned with the power of the human mind. Like a child or a puppy, the mind must be trained. Because of its tendency to run wild, New Thought philosopher Ralph Waldo Emerson urged "*standing guard* at the portal of your mind." As humans, we are shaped by our beliefs. "We become what we think" is a core teaching of Science of Mind. The goal of Buddhism is to *awaken* to our true Buddha nature and become enlightened during this lifetime. In both traditions, the emphasis is on unfolding the true potential of a human life by discarding ingrained beliefs and patterns of behavior that do not serve us. This process requires both a desire to change and making a commitment to a change process.

My life would have been dramatically different if, as a child, I had been taught about my potential to achieve my true Buddha nature, which is love. Instead, in the Lutheran Church, I was taught to believe that I was "by nature sinful and unclean" and will be judged by a supernatural being who lives in heaven.

Lutheran guilt became ingrained in my belief system and remains buried in my subconscious to this day.

About fifty years ago, my break from viewing myself as a Christian occurred when I read *Honest to God* by Anglican bishop John A.T. Robinson.[11] It was his book that introduced me to Paul Tillich's assertion that God is the "ground of our being." As Tillich predicted, his theology did in fact shake my theological foundations. It was a transformational moment in my life. Tillich's emphasis on *depth* created a paradigm shift in my thinking. To this day, I have an aversion to the word 'God.'

After "worshipping" at the altar of the Sunday *New York Times* for many years, I became a member of Jubilee Community church, in Asheville, North Carolina. One Sunday, Howard Hanger, the founding minister, told the congregation, "Christianity repels me, the historic Jesus Christ compels me." The message spoke to me because I no longer identified as a Christian.

After leaving the Christian tradition, my twenty-five-year search had many twists and turns including going with Margaret to Siddha Yoga ashrams in the New York Catskills and India in an attempt to keep my marriage alive. At the ashram, I was exposed to the Hindu belief that "God dwells within you as you; see God in each other." This "definition" of God still rings true to me. However, unlike my wife, I never bought into needing a guru.

After our divorce, I took workshops in the teachings of the Buddha and found secular Buddhism, which has no concept of a Supreme Being and thus lacks the duality of God and man. At this point in my life, I see myself as a non-theist. Buddhism

---

11 Robinson, John A.T., *Honest to God* (Philadelphia: The Westminster Press, 1963).

is sometimes referred to as the "middle path," which requires action instead of beliefs. It is based on four noble truths that Siddhartha Gautama awakened to 2,500 years ago— (1) life contains anguish (2) which is caused by cravings and ignorance, and (3) the cessation of anguish (4) by following an eightfold dharma path that leads to enlightenment.

My active practice as a secular Buddhist ended when I moved to a Quaker retirement community and attended Quaker meetings for two years until I left the community. When I met Mary Anne, a retired Unity minister, my spiritual life turned to New Thought. With no Unity congregation in northern Delaware, Mary Anne introduced me to Science of Mind, a similar New Thought group. I now see myself as a secular Buddhist, who sees much of value in New Thought philosophy, which I find compliments the teachings of the Buddha. As stated above, both promote understanding the human mind. According to Buddhist psychology, learning to love is an ongoing process in a life that is subject to change. Love is not a goal or a destination but a way of life—what one does. Living a human life requires accepting the reality of a flow of events that may cause anguish and pain.

Two takeaways from Buddhist psychology are: (1) the romantic notion of "marital bliss" is not a realistic goal because we live in a contingent (subject to change) world. And (2) knowing and accepting suffering while working to let go of craving (which causes the suffering) is an ongoing pursuit. I believe that being in a loving relationship is superior to a monastic life in gaining release from suffering because of the many opportunities to experience suffering and heal from it. Realistically, each of us has *wants* that our partner is unable or unlikely to satisfy. And our partner is also a suffering human being. In learning to love, accepting both of these realities is critical. And, as we will explore later, a loving relationship can heal wounds from childhood and from previous relationships. Both the teachings of the Buddha and New Thought philosophy view this healing as one's lifework.

Awakening our Buddha nature is a way of describing enlightenment. In the awakened mind, there is no concept of an unchanging self that is separate from oneness with others. Until we experience a sense of oneness, our human limitations make it almost impossible for any of us to really love another as we love ourselves. Therefore, we must accept the truth that love lies within us as our birthright and it is natural to express it. From a Buddhist perspective, love overcomes the cravings of the rational mind by opening the mystical mind state. *Metta*, or loving kindness, is a Buddhist practice that promotes working toward the well-being of both oneself and others.

A Piece of the Puzzle

Awakening our Buddha nature results from practicing loving kindness and generosity. In the awakened mind, there is no concept of a separate unchanging self. "Change your thinking, change your life" is a core teaching of Science of Mind spiritually.

Nature *and* Nurture

I believe an infant is born with Buddha nature. Joy, love, and spontaneity are the essence of an infant. If raised in a healthy family, the vulnerable infant learns to trust his/her connection to one or more loving, nurturing caregivers. This fortunate infant has an open heart, a feeling of acceptance, and is free to express the full range of human emotions. In explaining his

Mexican Toltec understanding of life in *The Four Agreements*, Don Miguel Ruiz asserts that expressing and receiving love is part of being a normal human.[12] This assertion is based on his observation of infants who are not afraid to love. But then what the Toltec call domestication (i.e., conditioning) occurs. Our natural ability to love diminishes and we become a shadow of our real selves; we do not accept and love the unique beings that we are.

As a child grows, a process called "individuation" takes place and a unique personality emerges. However, this personality is not fixed; by changing our *perspective,* our personality can be changed. *Learning to love* is based on this premise. If love is the core reality of every human being, our true *nature*, we are capable of awakening to it through a process of incremental change. The word "recovery" as used in twelve-step programs connotes becoming more like the being we were at birth, naturally expressing our Christ consciousness or Buddha nature.

At one time *tabula rasa was* the belief that the human mind was a clean slate before ideas were imprinted on it. But this theory has been found to be fundamentally wrong. Research has shown that babies are born with strong predispositions that affect personality and behavior. This reflects the unique set of genes each infant inherited. Nurture which can be loving, indifferent, or even abusive fills in the personality. Abuse occurs in families, in institutions like the church or Boy Scouts. Bullying in social media has become rampant. For many, being a child today is not easy.

Thus, the human psyche that emerges from childhood is a product of both nature *and* nurture. But which is more

---

12 Ruiz, Don Miguel *The Four Agreements* (San Rafael, CA: Amber-Allen Publishing, 1997).

important? In his book *Blueprint: How DNA Makes Us Who We Are,* King's College London professor of behavioral genetics Robert Plomin argues that recent genetic research has concluded that the dominant twentieth century emphasis on *nurture* (who we become is determined largely by our family experiences) is wrong.[13] Although such experiences affect us, Plomin contends that we bounce back to our genetic trajectory from these environmental "bumps." In his book, Plomin asserts that psychological differences between people are explained largely by genetics. This was a revolutionary idea to me when I read the book. And, as I stated in the Foreword, much of my book was written before reading *Blueprint,* and therefore, sometimes contains inconsistencies resulting from my evolving understanding of the human experience as I wrote the book.

Pause and Ponder: *Does Plomin's assertion about the long-term importance of your DNA in "who you are" ring true to you? Write about it citing personal examples.*

With my new perspective on the importance of nature, I finally recognize and acknowledge inheriting cognitive abilities that allowed me to succeed in my academic career and in writing this book. My father, who died fifty years ago, took pride in having only a sixth-grade education. I don't recall him ever reading a book. Creating successful businesses was his calling in life; our careers could not have been more different. However, genetically I believe we are quite similar and I am indebted to his DNA for abilities that allowed me to succeed in the life I chose. In the process of writing this book, I've concluded that I'm very much like my father. Having read about

---

13   Plomin, Robert, *Blueprint: How DNA Makes Us Who We Are* (Cambridge, MA: The MIT Press, 2018).

my upbringing in Chapter 1, the last statement may astound you as it astounds me that I am making it. As you may recall, I was told, and always believed, that I was like my mother. This demonstrates the importance of keeping our minds open to new perspectives. To be accurate, my life is a blend of the characteristics of both of my parents and the extent to which each parent impacted my childhood.

A recent dream confirms my new perspective that in important ways, I'm *not* "just like my mother" as I was programmed to believe as a child. In the dream, a dead woman wakes up and begins to move her arms and gets out of her casket, but then gets back into the casket. Later in the dream, another woman is wheeling the casket to the front door of the funeral parlor and "the dead woman" gets out and leaves.

This dream is about a woman leaving the funeral home. I left the funeral home when I went to college, but its shadow followed me. As I pondered the dream, it occurred to me that the image of a woman walking out the funeral home door was about my belief that I'm just like my mother. This realization allowed my true masculinity (being like my father) to emerge. As a result of insights about the importance of *nature* and my interpretation of this dream, I am revising the perspective on "who I am" that I have carried for more than eight decades.

One of the insights I received from Plomin's book is that my history of anxiety and depression may come from my DNA. Plomin contends that it's hard to identify any psychological experience completely devoid of genetic influence. It seems likely that my three bouts of clinical depression would not have occurred had I not created experiences that I couldn't cope with—becoming a father, divorce, and leaving a relationship to move to a retirement community. Our DNA, of course, also shows up in our bodies. My baldness comes from both gene pools—my father and my three maternal uncles were all bald.

To round out this discussion on nature *and* nurture, we will explore the role that *fear* plays in the human experience. When I did a word check of the first three chapters of the manuscript, the word *fear* showed up continuously in my life story. People who are afraid attempt to control their external environments, including their relationships. Confronting and openly discussing our fears allows love to emerge in an ongoing process of growth and connection.

Pause and Ponder: *What are you still afraid of? Create a list of your fears, and as you become conscious of new fears, add them to the list. Do your fears inhibit your ability to love?*

My Abilities

At age sixty-four, when I retired from college teaching, I took the Highlands Abilities Battery to seek a direction for the next chapter in my life. The results of the test revealed that I have outstanding *concept organization* and good *idea productivity*. I also scored above average on observation and "time frame orientation." Time frame orientation reflects my ability to set goals, plan actions, and accomplish tasks. These abilities contributed to success in my academic career. On the other hand, I scored in the low range in both visual speed and accuracy— the ability to interpret written symbols quickly and accurately. This deficiency explains why I tend to be a slow reader and did poorly on timed IQ tests. Each of us has unique strengths and weaknesses. We must capitalize on our strengths without comparing ourselves to others who excel in areas that are not our strengths.

When he interpreted my test results, a psychologist said I would not be happy unless I was using my driving abilities—concept organization and idea generation. He was right. In retirement, writing this book has given new meaning to my life.

In conclusion, much of what I have written in the first two chapters of the book concerns the impact of nurture—especially experiences in childhood and my marriage—on my eight-seven-year journey. Thus, the book has a largely "nurture" perspective. You will find sections where I present myself as a *victim* of my unusual childhood. Reading *Blueprint* gave me a better understanding of my unique *nature*. After reading the book, reviewing the results of the Highlands Battery took on new meaning for me. The thesis of Act 1 is that we must know ourselves before we can change. The challenges of changing oneself will be discussed in Act 2. Fortunately, much of what we can change is not hardwired into our brains. As discussed in the Foreword, it is based on our point of view, our perspective. I encourage you to be open to constantly examine, and when appropriate, revise your perspective.

Pause, Ponder, and Write: *We are all gifted with a unique set of abilities, skills, and potentials. Are you aware of your unique gifts? What are they? Are you cultivating and using them? Take some time to write your answers to these questions.*

Do Humans Have Souls?

Many people believe that as humans, we have souls. While difficult to define, one view is that the soul resides in the "ground of our being," using Paul Tillich's term. In a mystical mind state, an individual becomes intuitively aware of the soul. Our minds and our souls differentiate humans from other animal species. The mind is often associated with the brain; the concept of body-mind connection will be explored later in the book. In Christianity, the soul is considered to be immortal and may go to heaven. In Hinduism, the soul is eternal and reincarnates from one being to another. On the other hand, secular Buddhism has no concept of a soul that outlives human existence. Love requires developing a consciousness of our inherent *oneness* with others. An individual can view his/her world from either (1) a point of separation or (2) a point of oneness. The concept of being separate suggests a duality, which in Buddhist thinking, is an illusion. This consciousness of our inherent oneness with others cannot be limited to a significant other, family, and friends. Oneness extends to all humanity, including people from different ethnicities. My perspective changed when I became a mentor to first and second grade African-American boys in a largely segregated inner city school. I now understand my unconscious racism and the impact of racism in our country.

A Piece of the Puzzle

Who we are results from interactions between our DNA and our life experiences—our nature and our nurture. To a great extent, our life experiences define who we think we are. *Learning to love* requires getting in touch with the purity of our nature at birth.

Transition

This chapter is about transforming yourself. However, first you must know yourselves. Therefore, the next part of the book is about self-discovery. By taking the time to write when prompted to do so, you are likely to find that you know yourself much better when you finish this chapter. We progress from discussing some general characteristics of being human to exploring five conditions that can become barriers to love: (1) the demonic, (2) protective shells, (3) the egoic mind, (4) addictions, and (5) values. As you read the following, please look at your own life.

Act 2. Scene 1. Changing Yourself: Acknowledging Barriers to Love

Acknowledge the Demonic

As recorded in Matthew 16:23 in the New International Version of the Christian Bible, Jesus turned to Peter, and said, "Get behind me, Satan! You are a stumbling block to me; you do not have in mind the concerns of God, but merely human concerns." From this statement, I conclude that Jesus recognized a demonic force and equated it to the egoic mind.

In *Living with the Devil: A Meditation on Good and Evil,* Stephen Batchelor lays out the Buddhist notion that identifies the devil (Mara) as anything obstructive in life.[14] However, Mara also serves us because frustrations provide incentives to break out of our ruts and change. Conversely, living in the grip of the demonic has the potential to result in evil behavior.

We must acknowledge and accept the existence of negative thoughts and feelings that pop up, often randomly, in our conscious minds. But instead of identifying with them, view them as transitory visits from our dark side and recognize that they will pass if we do not create a sense of self out of them. The demonic influenced even the Buddha after waking up to his

---

14 Batchelor, Stephen, *Living with the Devil* (New York: Riverhead Books, 2004).

true essence—loving kindness. Thus, Buddhism recognizes the reality of the demonic as part of the human condition that must be confronted if one is to break free of it.

Hints about the existence of my my unique demons periodically show up in my dreams. A recent dream provides an example. In the dream, I'm with my partner at a church social event and go looking for her when I'm ready to leave. I find her dancing with another man. In the dream, a bystander comments, "They're dancing awfully close." In the next scene, I find her in a small room, where the man is demonstrating a string trick to her. When I go to kiss her, she turns away and ignores me. When I awoke from the dream, I was quite anxious. As I have learned to interpret dreams, this dream is not about Mary Anne; it's about various aspects of me. I believe my fear of abandonment showed up in the dream. This fear could go back to never bonding with my mother and/or events in my marriage. Feeling insecure seems to be one of my demons.

In another dream, I've run into numerous "roadblocks." In the beginning, I was told that I can't park in the parking lot. Then I was told that I can't eat in the restaurant. This process continued with my path blocked at every turn by a group of "goons" that I found threatening. In the process, my life shrinks because of fear. I eventually wound up working in a menial job in a church. As I pondered the dream, I concluded that it represents demons that restrict my life experience, making it somewhat comparable to living in a straightjacket.

Pause and Ponder: *Can you relate to living in a straightjacket at times?*

Recently, we went to a restaurant with another couple to celebrate Mary Anne's birthday. When we got to the restaurant's outdoor dining area, we were seated next to a table of seven or eight noisy women. When Mary Anne asked to be moved to another table, we were told that all tables were reserved. When Jan and Steve arrived a few minutes later, Jan also suggested that we get a table away from the noisy women. Rather than explaining the situation to her, I said forcefully, "Shut up, Jan." During the remainder of the lunch, I was somewhat loud, a dramatic departure from my usual quiet demeanor. Two weeks later, I realized that I needed to apologize to Jan for my rude behavior. She accepted my apology with grace. I believe the situation unleashed a demon long buried in my subconscious. Could it be a belated rebellion against needing to be quiet as a child? Or repressed anger toward my ex-wife, who never participated in planning trips, but became critical of the plan when we were on our way? Or was my aggressive behavior stimulated by the noise in the atmosphere? Possibly all three. Some people experience multiple personalities. Am I one of them? If so, my quest is to uncover a less serious Jim.

Pause and Ponder: *What demons block your path forward in life?*

A Piece of the Puzzle

As humans, we have a dark side, which is the antithesis of love. When our demons occur, we must be wary of creating an identity, a sense of *I am*, out of them. Simply recognize your demons for what they are—fleeting images from your dark side—and let them fade away.

Know Your Protective Shell

At times, I experience anxiety and tightness in my chest when I'm physically close to Mary Anne; I don't believe the anxiety has anything to do with my relationship with her. I believe that my chest tightness is a response to my fear of intimacy, a fear that I will be found inadequate sexually. I believe sexual incompatibility in my marriage may have led to my fear of intimacy. Therefore, fear of intimacy is part of my protective shell. Mary Anne, of course, has her own protective shell resulting from events in her life; her protective shell will be discussed in the section on "Know Your Partner."

A protective shell is a reaction to fear, which is both a learned emotion, and I believe, part of one's DNA. Apparently, babies begin to experience fear at about six months with separation anxiety occurring at a primal level when a caregiver they have formed a primary attachment to is not close-by. As a child grows up, he/she faces many scary situations, some of them traumatic. All of these experiences remain in the body-mind as stored emotions. These repressed emotions in the body-mind may emerge when the reactive mind state is in control, which, as we have learned, is most of the time.

Fear of rejection underlies social anxiety, which causes some people to avoid social situations. Many people use alcohol and/or drugs to anesthetize the fear. As an introvert, in my days of attending faculty cocktail parties, I never strayed far from the bar or the punch bowl. I had my last drink twenty years ago and now seldom attend social gatherings where I don't know anyone.

A panic reaction is an extreme form of anxiety, one that I experienced as department chairman when I was thrust into situations outside of my comfort zone. Hosting guests from the business community at an event is an example. When experiencing a panic attack, I had to breathe deeply to restore my equanimity. An extreme form of anxiety is post-traumatic stress disorder (PTSD) suffered by soldiers and others who have experienced major trauma. Each person, of course, brings a unique protective shell to a relationship.

In contemplating our human protective shell, the lobster is a good metaphor. A lobster grows a shell to protect it from predators. As the lobster grows, each year it sheds its shell and grows a new, larger one. I believe humans also have an invisible shell that tends to separate them from other human beings. With each fearful experience we live through, the shell grows thicker. Clearly, having a thick shell creates a barrier to building a trusting, loving relationship. At the extreme, it results in a clinical maladjustment termed paranoia.

The question is whether humans can shed their thick shell and grow a new one that is more accepting and loving. I believe this takes time as a relationship matures and trust develops. The incidence of divorce in the United States illustrates that many couples are incapable of adjusting to each other. It also indicates that many individuals are not motivated to change—to grow a loving skin to replace their fearful shell. In other words, they are not willing to learn to love.

As we live together, I find that Mary Anne is coming out of her introverted shell. When we walk together in a park, she often greets people we pass and makes comments like "I see your dogs are taking you for a walk." This is not the behavior of an introvert. I see the emergence of her authentic, friendly self. Living together, we both feel accepted for who we are and we each feel our partner's love. Mary Anne often tells me that I am the only man who ever said, "I love you" to her. As we learn to trust each other, we are slowly shedding our protective shells in our relationship.

This section on protective shells is incomplete without a discussion on anger—an emotion that works against creating a loving relationship. As I conducted a search of the manuscript for the word "anger," I found it repeatedly in the first two chapters—"growing up over the funeral home" and "my marriage to Margaret." In addition to being afraid of the anger of others, I know that I carry a lot of repressed anger that I must acknowledge and learn to cope with.

Pause and Ponder: *Contemplate your unique protective shell. Can it be attributed to fear? Anger? Both? What life experiences do you attribute it to?*

A Piece of the Puzzle

Like a lobster, we develop shells to protect us. As we build trust in a relationship, our fears and repressed anger fade and love emerges. Loving relationships have the capacity to heal our wounds and dissolve our shells.

Know Your Egoic Mind

The meaning of ego is a conundrum that puzzled me for years. The first part of life is about differentiation—creating a sense of "I". But, according to Eckhart Tolle, that sense of "I" becomes distorted, thereby creating an egoic mind, which is self-absorbed. In a relationship, the transition from "I" to "we" begins with generosity—the first practice of the Buddhist path to enlightenment. This process, as I see it, is moving from dependence as an infant, to independence as a young adult, to interdependence in a relationship without becoming codependent by surrendering one's sense of "I" and living a life dedicated to pleasing someone else.

The egoic mind is a major barrier to love. As mentioned elsewhere, one of my psychotherapists had this sign over his desk, "I'd rather be loving than right." The following is an example where my reactive mind was not loving. At the beginning of a semester, an Asian student showed up in my Lifelong Learning class; she was not on my class list and insisted that she had added the class. Having less than ten minutes to rearrange the chairs in the room and get my thoughts together to start the class, I was completely caught up in my own drama. Lacking empathy for the student's feelings, I abruptly told her to leave the room and talk to whoever admitted her to my class which was closed to additional students. Within five minutes, the program director came to my classroom to inform me that I had traumatized the student who came to her office in tears. As it turned out, she had been added to a different section of the course. As I pondered my rude behavior, I lost sleep. I now realize that taking time to help the student was the loving thing to do and clearly more important than getting my class started on time. Instead, I hurt another human being.

Pause and ponder: *Can you recall having a similar reactive experience in your life that you later regretted? Were you caught up in your own drama?*

Returning to the meaning of "ego," in Freudian theory, *ego strength* helps individuals maintain emotional stability as they cope with internal and external stress. The Freudian ego represents the ability to deal effectively with the demands of the id (the primal mind) and the superego (the sense of right and wrong in the rational mind). In this sense, the ego plays a positive role in adapting to life. In 1993, George Valliant, Professor of Psychiatry at Harvard Medical School, published *The Wisdom of the Ego*. In the introduction, Valliant states that there is a world of difference between being self-centered (being egotistical) and being centered in the self (possessing ego strength).[15]

Matt Kahn and Jon Kabat-Zinn have also addressed the problem of being ego-centric. A barrier to love arises when one is inflicted by what Matt Kahn terms "ego inflammation"—self-centered reactions to events. The title of Kahn's book is *Whatever Arises, Love That: A Love Revolution That Begins with You*.[16] Although it may be difficult, Kahn proposes that we accept the flow of life's events and also recognize our inflamed reactions to events that arise. By accepting reality, we can learn from any situation, however upsetting it may be.

Becoming aware of our reactions is the first step in changing our behavior. In a video on Matt Kahn.org, Kahn expands on "whatever arises, love that" with this five-step prescription to overcome judgments: (1) Nothing is stupid, (2) Everything helps everything, (3) If it could have happened another way, it would have, (4) We manifest things to strengthen a weakness, and (5) Thank you.[17]

Pause and Ponder: *What is your understanding of each step of Kahn's five-step prescription to overcome judgments? How can you apply it in your life?*

---

15 Valliant, George, *The Wisdom of the Ego* (Cambridge, MA: Harvard University Press, 1993).

16 Khan, Matt, *Whatever Arises, Love That: A Love Revolution That Begins with You* (Boulder, CO: Sounds True, 2016).

17 Matt Kahn.org.

In summary, I believe Kahn is saying that much of the flow of life is beyond the control of the desires of our egoic minds and that painful experiences contribute to our growth, but rejecting them causes additional pain. Khan concludes that love is stronger than anything. We might paraphrase a twelve-step saying with "let go and let love," which is our true *nature*.

In *Wherever You Go, There You Are,* mindfulness teacher Jon Kabat-Zinn contends that "I," "me," and "mine" are parts of our thinking. One Buddhist teacher calls this "selfing"—that inevitable and incorrigible tendency to construct out of almost everything and every situation, an "I," a "me," and a "mine," and to operate in the world from that limited perspective.[18] Kabat-Zinn cites examples: *my* child, *my* way, *my* house, *my* opinion, *my* future. If you leave one relationship for another, you take yourself to the new one—this is the thesis of Kabat-Zinn's book. Therefore, before entering into a new relationship, the challenge is to change yourself. After my divorce, my therapist told me to remain celibate for a year to heal. Before long I entered into a platonic relationship with a woman I met at a retreat. The relationship was her idea and after a year, she ended it.

Many years ago, I had a neighbor who turned every conversation to himself; Al seemed to lack empathy and the ability to listen. I found this an extreme case of how our worlds revolve around our egos. Frank, another friend, was almost the polar opposite of Al. To the best of his ability, Frank told me he avoids using the word "I."

In *Confessions of a Buddhist Atheist,* Stephen Batchelor discusses the Buddhist concept of "emptiness of self." In Buddhist thinking, nothing is fixed at the core of one's identity

---

18 Kabat-Zinn, Jon, *Wherever You Go, There You Are: Mindfulness Meditation in Everyday Life* (New York: Hyperion, 1994, 2005).

as a person.[19] Recognition of this truth allows one to change. But such deep and fundamental change runs up against our inflamed ego that wants everything to go its way. We must develop the ability to view events from the perspective of others rather than just ourselves. This is called empathy.

The existence of life after death is a mystery. In the same way, the dimensions that love will take following the retreat of the self-absorbed ego is a also mystery. We must be willing to experience that mystery with an open mind. If we can enter into a loving relationship without expectations and preconceptions, the relationship has a greater opportunity to thrive. Let love emerge and grow organically and trust that the process is guided by an intelligence beyond your rational mind. Instead of trying to figure it out, listen to your intuition, which comes from a deeper level of consciousness. Loving relationships grow when both parties are able to "go with the flow." Relationships break down and a power struggle emerges when one or both parties try to control the process.

Pause and Ponder: *Does self-absorption inhibit your ability to have a loving relationship? Write about some examples from your past.*

A Piece of the Puzzle

The human ego represents a primary barrier to love. Eckhart Tolle wrote about the "egoic mind" and Matt Kahn talked about ego inflammation, "I," "me," and "mine" thinking. A loving relationship is based on creating an "our" perspective while also building up each partner's unique individual identities.

---

19 Batchelor, Stephen, *Confessions of a Buddhist Atheist* (New York: Spiegel and Grau Trade Paperbacks, 2011).

Know Your Addictions

This wisdom from Rumi provides a foundation for this book: "Your task is not to seek for love, but merely to seek and find all the barriers within yourself that you have built up against it."[20] Some of these barriers are the result of unconscious reactions and/or addictions that run our lives. We are familiar with addictions to substances like alcohol and drugs. But what is an addiction? According to Wikipedia: "Addiction is a *brain disorder* characterized by compulsive [behavior] in rewarding stimuli despite adverse consequences."

The success of Alcoholics Anonymous (AA), which was founded in 1935, has spawned a plethora of programs patterned on its twelve steps. The thirty-four programs listed in Wikipedia include seven for people addicted to a substance including alcohol, narcotics, heroin, and prescription pain pills. A second group is for family members, who have been or are impacted by living with an addict. These include Al-Anon/Alateen, which is associated with AA. Although the impact of all forms of addiction creates barriers to love, substance abuse is not the primary focus of this book. As you read the following list, check those that may relate to your life experience. The ones you checked may be your addictions.

- ACA—Adult Children of Alcoholics, for those who were raised in alcoholic or other dysfunctional families.

- Al-Anon/Alateen, for friends and families of alcoholics.

---

20 Rumi, *op. cit.*

- CoDA—Co-Dependents Anonymous, for people working to end patterns of dysfunctional relationships and develop healthy ones.
- DA—Debtors Anonymous.
- EA—Emotions Anonymous, for recovery from emotional and mental illness.
- GA—Gamblers Anonymous.
- OA—Overeaters Anonymous and FA—Food Addicts in Recovery Anonymous.
- SLAA—Sex and Love Addicts Anonymous and SCA—Sexual Compulsions Anonymous.
- SIA—Survivors of Incest Anonymous.
- UA—Underearners Anonymous.
- WA—Workaholics Anonymous.

Over the years, I have attended many meetings of ACA and CoDA and a few meetings of Al-Anon. I have imagined creating a group called ACOW—Adult Children of Workaholics. Although it doesn't affect me, with the current obesity crisis, I see the need for UEA—Unhealthy Eaters Anonymous.

As a human being living in this culture, you may have checked one or more of the above addictions. You can learn more about groups that speak to you by going to their websites. The statement "you are not alone" is likely to appear there. Attending a twelve-step meeting allows one to talk to an understanding audience about his/her unique life experiences, and equally important, to listen to the experiences of others who are in recovery from the addiction. Because finding a local group to explore your addiction may be difficult, check for online meetings. We will explore the twelve-step process later in Act 2.

Pause and Ponder: *Which of the above twelve-step recovery groups can you relate to? Describe your addictive behavior.*

A Piece of the Puzzle

Addictions are unconscious manifestations of our "stuff" that may create barriers to love. The process of recovering from an addiction begins with owning it.

Know Your Values

"The Quest for a Moral Life" is the subtitle of *The Second Mountain* by David Brooks.[21] Let's contemplate the meaning of a *moral life*. The word "morality" connotes standards of right and wrong. Brooks makes a distinction between a life lived for self and a life lived to benefit others. According to Brooks, although our culture may value the former, living that life does not always bring satisfaction. As noted earlier, at eighty-seven, generativity is a guiding value in my life. Rather than spending my discretionary income on myself, I use it to benefit my children and grandchildren.

To what extent are the teachings of the Buddha relevant in our egocentric Western culture today? In *Loving Kindness*, Buddhist meditation teacher Sharon Salzberg relates the story of a meditation master from Thailand. During a visit to the United States, he observed that in the West, the emphasis of Buddhist practice seems to be meditation first, then morality, with teaching about generosity being almost an afterthought.[22] This is the opposite of the classical sequence of [Buddhist] teachings and

21 Brooks, David, *The Second Mountain* (New York: Random House, 2019).

22 Salzberg, Sharon, *Loving Kindness* (Boston: Shambhala, 2001).

practice in Asia, which begins with generosity, then morality (loving kindness), and then meditation or insight. Salzberg also observed that, to the Buddha, a generous heart was the keystone of the awakened mind. Since a generous heart connotes a loving heart, Salzberg seems to be equating a "true spiritual life" with love.

Microsoft co-founder Bill Gates provides an example of redefining one's life purpose. At 45, Gates and his wife created the Bill and Melinda Gates Foundation to invest his Microsoft billions in projects to relieve the suffering and improve the lives of less fortunate people around the world. As a result of Bill Gates changing his focus from managing a large corporation to managing the Gates Foundation, the lives of people around the world are being transformed.

As mentioned earlier, my life changed when I became a school mentor. In the training to become a mentor, I learned about the dismal situation in the largely segregated Wilmington elementary schools, where the mostly African-American students are dramatically behind those in suburban schools in academic achievements. In one mentor training class, Judy Govatos, a classmate who became a friend, suggested that I read The New Jim Crow by Michelle Alexander. The book presents a bleak picture of the mistreatment of African-Americans in the criminal justice system in the United States.[23] Judy and I decided to create a course to explore the issue and were fortunate to enroll Bebe Coker, a civil rights icon in Delaware, to join us. At Osher Lifelong Learning, the three of us developed and offered two courses: "Legalized Racism in the United States" and "Racism, Can We Talk?" I finally had a cause—raising aware-

---

23 Alexander, Michelle, The New Jim Crow (New York: The New Press, 2011).

ness of racism and making a difference, one child at a time, in inner-city public schools in Wilmington. However, enrolling others to step out of their comfort zones and become mentors has been challenging. People are more interested in *discussing* social justice than they are in engaging in social action.

Pause and ponder: *What are your core values? Is generosity one of them? Or, do you value greed?*

A Piece of the Puzzle

Our values determine how we use our time and resources, with generosity and greed being polar opposites. The latter is a major barrier to love.

Act 2. Scene 2. Changing Yourself: Overcoming Barriers to Love

Preface

If you have made a decision that you want to change by addressing the barriers to love that have developed over your lifetime, Act 2 presents a number of approaches to facilitate change. I'll begin with a personal experience.

Change

A few months ago, I met a friend I had last seen more than thirty years ago. Bob and I first met in a Reevaluation Counseling group where we worked together as co-counselors; we knew each other pretty well. After talking for a few minutes in our chance encounter, Bob remarked, "You've been transformed." This caused me to ponder Bob's remark. Since I had last seen him, I'm more than twenty years into retirement and have had almost twenty years to heal from my divorce. I've attended numerous twelve-step meetings and several Buddhist retreats. I'm in a relationship that is working and writing a book about love. I'm pleased that Bob recognized a "new" Jim.

Let Go of Your Egoic Mind to Renew Your Life

If the egoic mind is the biggest barrier to giving and receiving love, what can be done about it? As the adage goes, "old habits die hard" because each of us lives in a rut that tends to get deeper and deeper. As you adopt loving kindness as your North Star, your heart begins to open. Dramatic change takes time and practice, of course. Letting go of a self-centered mind-set requires: (1) a belief that you can change, (2) a desire and intention to change, and (3) finding and following a path such as Buddhism or a twelve-step recovery program. This is a mystical process, which cannot be accomplished by the rational mind. In twelve-step recovery programs, the second step, "Came to believe that a power greater than ourselves can return us to sanity," provides the path which requires faith in a power higher than our egoic rational mind. Letting of an egocentric mind is a lifelong process that can lead to moments of enlightenment.

A Piece of the Puzzle

Being self-centered, the rational mind creates a barrier to love. Purposeful change requires (1) making a commitment to a path and (2) faith in a power greater than yourself. This is a mystical (not a rational) process.

Change Your Values to Renew Your Life

Please reflect on and answer these questions:

- How do you use your free time?
- Are you generous?
- Are you greedy?
- How do you spend your disposable income?
- Do you have a sense of entitlement?
- Are you concerned about people less fortunate than you?
- If you are Caucasian, are you aware of white privilege—the many benefits that accrue to you because of the color of your skin?
- If you are a man, are you aware of the benefits of male privilege in our patriarchal culture?
- Do you have an appreciation consciousness?
- Is your life guided by a moral code?
- Do you see other people as objects to use for your benefit?
- Are you fair-minded?

Your answers to the above questions reflect your personal values, which are shaped by your attitudes and beliefs. I'm sure you could add to the list. Let's assume that your answers constitute a moral inventory of your life. To become more loving, are there dimensions of your life you desire to change? Our values guide our actions—how we use our time, talents, and resources. In the Book of Acts, Jesus is quoted as saying, "It is more blessed to give than to receive." According to the King James Version of the Bible that I grew up with, in 1st Corinthians 13:30, Paul said "And now abideth faith, hope, charity, these three; but the greatest of these is charity." In later versions of the Bible, the word "charity" was translated as "love". In discussing values, I prefer the word "charity" because it suggests generosity. One can be charitable by volunteering or giving money to worthy causes. I support a number of causes including the Hunger Project, which empowers people in Africa and elsewhere to become self-sufficient. However, as noted previously, my life changed when I stepped out of my comfort zone and became a mentor to second graders in an inner-city public school. This behavior change gave me an entirely new perspective on the impact of racism in America and my own racism. As a result, I now support the Southern Poverty Law Center, an organization that challenges racism in our country.

A Piece of the Puzzle

Before we can change our values, we must recognize and question them. Are they egocentric or generous and loving?

Release Trapped Emotions to Renew Your Life

Up to this point, I have skirted around a critical aspect of human behavior that has run my life subconsciously. Feelings and emotions were seldom addressed in my decades of psycho-therapy, which concentrated on the mind and largely ignored the body. Answering the question, "What are you thinking?" is easy for me, but I usually go blank when asked, "What are you feeling?"

As child, I learned to stuff my emotions. And, in doing research for this book, I have learned that repressed emotions remain in my body, and to some extent, subconsciously run my life because my reactive mind is largely in charge. In my case, I believe repressed fear, sadness, and anger run my life subconsciously to some extent.

Pause and Ponder: *Can you relate to having repressed emotions? If so, what are they?*

In the first two chapters of the book, you have learned something about the origins of my *repressed* emotions. Cognitively, I know that I can only release them by emoting. To release my sadness, I must cry. To release my anger, I must scream. If I drop my inhibitions, yelling is easy for me. During the Hoffman Quadrinity Process, a training I did more than twenty years ago, I spent a week beating on a pillow with a wiffle-ball bat and screaming to release anger at my parents. However, recognizing that the body grieves and cannot be ordered to do so by the mind presents a challenge to releasing my deep sadness.

In England, Liz Adamson has written a series of small books, *The Ultimate Guides to Emotional Freedom.*[24] I have a copy of *Releasing Anger,* in which Adamson contends that one must recognize the source of the anger before safely releasing it. Adamson then prescribes these ways to release anger: verbal expression, physical expression, and purposeful deep breathing. During my marriage, I kept a set of dishes from Goodwill in my garage. When I needed to release anger, I threw them against the concrete block wall. Obviously, that was a physical expression but I don't recall screaming while doing so. It was better to release my anger in my garage than to lash out at my wife. However, I doubt that it got to the source of my anger, which I believe, predated my marriage.

---

24 Adamson, Liz, *Releasing Anger* (Aylesford, Kent, U.K.: Diviniti Publishing Ltd., 2000).

In his book, *The Tapping Solution*, Nick Ortner advocates tapping on specific meridian endpoints while focusing on negative emotions or physical sensations.[25] *Emotional freedom technique* is another name for tapping. The goal of tapping is to rewire the brain to calm the nervous system by employing principles of both ancient acupuncture and modern psychology. While one can learn Ortner's method at a weekend workshop or by reading his book, breaking free of troublesome emotions requires a commitment to practice tapping over a period of time. For instructions and demonstrations of tapping, Google *thetappingsolution.com/tapping101*. Be patient; it took years to bury the emotions in your body-mind. Although I have dabbled with tapping, I have not yet made the commitment necessary to gain emotional freedom. Doing so is on my agenda.

A Piece of the Puzzle

Because feelings and emotions tend to cause our reactions unconsciously, we must become conscious of our unique repressed emotions that create barriers to love. The only way to release feelings and emotions is to emote—something your body, not your rational mind, does.

Begin Recovery from Your Addictions to Renew Your Life

The following twelve steps are taken from Co-Dependents Anonymous[26]

---

25 Ortner, Nick, *The Tapping Solution* (Carlsbad, CA: Hay House, 2013).
26 Co-Dependents Anonymous, *In the Moment Daily Meditation Book, Second Edition* (Denver, NC: CoRe Publications, 2011).

1. We admitted that we are powerless over others, that our lives had become unmanageable.

2. Came to believe that a power greater than ourselves could restore us to sanity.

3. Made a decision to turn our will and our lives over to the care of God, as we understood God.

4. Made a searching and fearless moral inventory of ourselves.

5. Admitted to God, to ourselves, and to another human being the exact nature of our wrongs.

6. Were entirely ready to have God remove all these defects of character.

7. Humbly asked God to remove our shortcomings.

8. Made a list of persons we had harmed and became willing to make amends to them all.

9. Made direct amends to such people except when to do so would injure them or others.

10. Continued to take personal inventory and when we were wrong, promptly admitted it.

11. Sought through prayer and meditation to improve our constant contact with God as we understood God, praying only for knowledge of God's will for us and the power to carry that out.

12. Having had a spiritual awakening as a result of these steps, we tried to carry this message to other co-dependents and to practice these principles in all our affairs.

It's clear from the above that twelve-step recovery work is based upon faith "in a power greater than ourselves that could restore us to sanity." Believing this proposition requires a "leap of faith" in something bigger than our individual egos.

In twelve-step programs, recovery tends to begin when one hits rock-bottom and admits that his/her life has become unmanageable. Step one seems to work best when proclaimed before others in a meeting of individuals recovering from a similar addiction.

Although I have attended many Adult Children and Co-Dependents Anonymous meetings over the years, I have never worked the steps. In other words, I continue to see my life as manageable and refuse to surrender to a higher power. Obviously, my ego remains firmly in charge. As my life became seriously unmanageable when I became a father for the first time, I panicked. At that point, I put my faith in psychiatric treatment, which included tranquilizing medication, which allowed me to "recover" without dealing with the fear that caused my panic.

A Piece of the Puzzle

In the twelfth step of Co-Dependents Anonymous, "Having had a spiritual awakening as a result of these steps, we tried to carry this message to other codependents and to practice these principles in all our affairs," the emphasis shifts from personal growth to practicing loving kindness.

Recognize Your Demons to Renew Your Life

We all have a dark side as well as a light side. According to Stephen Batchelor, Mara (the Devil) continued to plague even the Buddha after he awoke and became enlightened. In our context, "and they lived happily ever after" happens in fairy tales but not in real life. A marriage inevitably includes pain and suffering as well as happiness.

If our demons represent our dark or negative side, they are a natural part of the dualism of life. As I see it, the trick is to accept the dualism of being human and not catastrophize when events are not going our way. When we catastrophize, our mood can descend into a deeper void. Rather than being black and white, life is shades of gray with occasional triumphs as well as apparent failures. It is a mistake to create a sense of self out of either extreme. Instead, accept that life has its ups and downs. Develop the perspective that any situation might be both bad and good rather than being one or the other. When demons arise, adopt "this too shall pass" as your mantra. Learn from your demons.

A Piece of the Puzzle

When events are not going the way desired by our egoic mind, accept this as the flow of life. As the stock market goes up and down, so do our psyches. Accept the inevitability of the dark side emerging in your life and know that it will pass. Learn from the demons in your life.

Still a Work in Progress

After more than four decades of psychotherapy and many twelve-step meetings, at eighty-seven, I remain a work in progress. This doesn't mean that I haven't changed. Quite the opposite. During the last thirty years, personal growth and change have been my mission. However, I still have fears that are barriers to love. To some extent, I am still afraid of women's anger, of being abandoned, of intimacy, and of my sexuality. I've been called stubborn. I believe my resistance to change is based on my egoic need to be right; I've made reference to this sign in one of my therapist's office: "I'd rather be loving than right."

Over my life span, I have changed my values dramatically. Today, as a secular Buddhist and progressive Democrat, I value generosity. However, fear, sadness, and anger remain as trapped emotions in my body. As stated before, with its emphasis on cognitive behavior, my years of psychotherapy largely ignored these emotions which are with me every day.

Although I never saw myself as an alcoholic, I was a daily drinker for decades until I stopped almost twenty years ago when I adopted a healthier diet. I've owned my shortcomings as a husband and have written to Margaret asking her for forgiveness. In her dying days, she has forgiven me. Our exchanges have been healing for both of us.

I'm beginning to accept my demons without creating a self out of thoughts that spontaneously arise. "This too shall pass" is a valuable tool for letting go of my dark side when it surfaces. When events do not go my way, I've learned to step beyond black and white thinking and to look for shades of gray. I accept the reality of situations by applying Matt Kahn's wisdom—"whatever arises, love that."

This book is only partially a product of my rational mind. Many of the insights that arise during the middle of the night or first thing in the morning are the product of the intuition of my mystical mind state. I have the genetic ability to organize concepts. This ability has served me well in both my academic career and in writing this book.

I grew up in a family where I never heard the word "love," and regrettably, don't recall saying "I love you" to my four children when they were young. As a result, believing that Mary

Anne loves me is sometimes challenging. Curiously, Mary Anne has comparable wounds from her childhood and marriage. Recognition of these wounds is the first step in healing them. I believe a divine force brought Mary Anne and me together to heal each other's wounds. Acknowledging and letting go of our *stuff* is a process like peeling an onion. As we get to know and confront our unique demons and addictions, increasingly, they don't unconsciously run our lives. I'm a much better partner than I was during my marriage. That, of course, is the goal of *learning to love.* I know I'm also a better father.

A Piece of the Puzzle

Having a partner who is also committed to personal growth and to creating a loving relationship is critical to the process of learning to love.

Pause and Ponder: *Act 2 presented five potential barriers to love in your life—(1) your egoic mind, (2) your values, (3) your trapped emotions, (4) your addictions, and (5) your demons. Rank them in the order in which they create barriers to love in your life. Meaningful change results from having a goal and making a commitment to achieve it. Beginning with your number one barrier, what is your goal to achieve change? For example, attending a twelve-step meeting is a good way to confront an addiction. Proceed with this process for your other barriers.*

Act 3. The Practice of Love
Preface

In Act 3, we turn to learning *how* to change our behavior. After recognizing the behaviors that serve as barriers to love, it's time to make a commitment to a *practice* of becoming a more loving person. Internalizing the Serenity Prayer is a good place to begin, followed by Matt Kahn's injunction—*whatever arises, love that.* Because of the human tendency to be dissatisfied with what one has and crave what one does not have, maintaining and growing a loving relationship is often a challenge. It requires commitment from both partners who may be recovering from wounds experienced in childhood or in previous relationships.

Embrace Internal Conflict: Holding the Tension of the Opposite

In *Alone with Others,* Stephen Batchelor observed that *being alone* and *being with* form the complex fabric of life.[27] As the title of his book suggests, human beings live with the paradoxical situation of being simultaneously *alone with others.* Thus, entering into a loving relationship inevitably results in internal tension. How much togetherness can we tolerate?

The egocentric mind and the loving heart represent opposites we all live with. Other opposites include being independent and being interdependent, clinging and aversion, desire and accepting reality. In *The Prophet,* Kahlil Gibran proclaimed, "When love beckons you, follow him, though his ways are hard and steep...For even as love crowns you, so shall he crucify you. Even as he is for your growth, so is he for your pruning."[28] Awareness and acceptance of life's contradictions is the key to breaking free of their hold on us. And, of course, recognize that

---

27 Batchelor, Stephen, *Alone with Others* (New York: Grove Press, 1983).

28 Gibran, Kahlil, *The Prophet* (New York: Albert A. Knopf Publisher, 1994) p. 11.

your partner brings his/her own unique tension of the opposites to the relationship.

In the words of theologian Reinhold Niebuhr, "The final wisdom of life requires *not* the annulment of incongruity, but the achievement of serenity within and about it."[29] Niebuhr was the author of the Serenity Prayer.

Pause and Ponder: *What are you taking away from this discussion of embracing internal conflict?*

A Piece of the Puzzle

Holding the tension of the opposites may be the biggest challenge that individuals face in a relationship. Awareness of your unique internal state and the courage and ability to communicate about the inevitable internal conflicts that arise is the key to the success of a relationship. Your partner, of course, is experiencing the same tension.

Know Your Partner, Accept Your Partner, Heal Your Partner

You may recall this wisdom of Viktor Frankl which provides a template for knowing your partner. "Love is the way to grasp another human being in the innermost core of his personality. By the spiritual act of love, he is enabled to see the essential traits and, even more, he/she sees that which is potential... [but] is not yet actualized. Furthermore, by his love, the loving person enables the beloved person to actualize these potentialities."[30] As you get to know your partner, accept this unique person who is different from you. Celebrate the differ-

---

29 Niebuhr, Reinhold (Quotations on-line).

30 Frankl, *op. cit.*

ences. Recognize that your partner probably carries wounds from childhood and/or previous relationships just as you do, and that your love can provide healing for those wounds.

Mary Anne has her own protective shell that, I believe, resulted from wounds incurred during childhood and her marriage. Her mother died a day after Mary Anne and her twin brother were born. For the first four years of their lives, Mary Anne and her brother lived with their father and her mother's sister and her husband, who were childless. Her bond with these parent figures was broken when her father remarried four years later. This transition was clearly a traumatic event at a critical juncture in Mary Ann's life; it haunts her to this day. One month before she turned twenty, Mary Anne married a man who was three years older. She met him when they worked in the same office during the summer between high school and college. The couple had three children during their twenty-three-year marriage that ended in divorce. In her forties, Mary Anne finally found her voice and was no longer willing to tolerate her dysfunctional marriage.

One morning, I asked Mary Anne, "Do you know how wonderful you are and how good you are for me? I am a different person than I was when we made the decision to share an apartment and our lives." Our love has been a healing experience for me as I believe it has been for Mary Anne as well. Mary Anne's sense of fulfillment is as important as mine. We complement and encourage each other. We have created something new in our life experiences—a loving relationship. We, of course, have the benefit of wisdom that comes from our life experiences.

Focused listening encourages sharing. In our more than four years together, Mary Anne and I have spent hundreds of hours in "pillow talk" sharing our life stories, especially our childhood wounds, which are amazingly similar. Understanding leads to empathy. Feeling heard and understood leads to healing and deepens love.

My marriage to Margaret might have lasted if I had understood and practiced Frankl's wisdom. Rather than encourage Margaret to develop her own life, I resisted it. Growing up in a patriarchy with an unconscious sense of male privilege, I was clueless when I married. And Margaret brought her own experience of living in a patriarchal family to our marriage.

A Piece of the Puzzle

As it requires conscious effort and time to understand yourself, a similar conscious effort must be made to know your partner's wounds and potential. The ability to listen without attempting to fix is the starting point in getting to know, accept, and heal your partner.

Creating a Conscious Relationship

Our first relationships are with our parents, siblings, extended family members, and other caregivers. As life progresses, we have relationships with friends, lovers, teachers, coaches, and in some cases, members of the clergy. The shadow of every relationship experience remains in our unconscious body-mind. The impact of my growing up in a patriarchal family is a good example.

Based on both his counseling and his study of couples, in 1988, Harville Hendrix reported his observations about the reality of marriages in *Getting the Love You Want,* his pioneering book on the dynamics of relationships.[31] Hendrix found that couples marry with the illusion of romantic love and with an unrealistic desire to live happily ever after. He also found that, as in my marriage, fear and anger cause couples to avoid intimacy. Hendrix believes that many marriages eventually evolve into a *power struggle.*

Hendrix identified two types of marriages: (1) the unconscious marriage and (2) the conscious marriage. Hendrix sees *childhood wounds* (or conditioning) as a cause of an *unconscious marriage.* Addressing and agreeing on the purpose of the union has the potential to reduce conflict in the relationship and also the divorce rate. This requires an ability to become aware of the unconscious desire to "have one's own way" and the willingness to compromise. When Mary Anne and I decided to share an apartment, we had a clear purpose. Being in our eighties, we wanted companionship, a commitment to take care of each other if required, and to learn to love.

During my marriage, I frequently heard Margaret say, "I don't like" or "I'm pissed." This should have been a signal for me to wake up and realize that Margaret had a different vision for our marriage than I did, but I was too self-absorbed to do so.

The Course of Love, a novel by Alain de Botton, chronicles the relationship of a woman from Scotland and a man from Beirut, Lebanon, two very different cultures.[32] While both are pursuing careers, they marry, and eventually have two demanding children. The result is a witches' brew of conflicting perspectives, hurt feelings, unmet needs, demands, and resentments.

---

31 Hendrix, Harville, *Getting the Love You Want* (New York: Henry Holt and Company, 1988).

32 de Botton, Alain, *The Course of Love* (New York: Simon & Schuster, 2016).

In his discussion of feedback, De Botton stresses the need for both parties to feel safe to critique the other's behavior before it morphs into resentment. This honest exchange fertilizes the ground for both the individuals and the relationship to bloom and grow; it is the opposite of a codependent relationship based on fear.

A relationship is an organic entity with a life of its own. If not nurtured, it will die. Because human beings bring complex conditioning to a relationship, creating a relationship is not a linear process—it has its ups and downs. And the downs can lead to higher ups if acknowledged and talked about. Relationships are an excellent opportunity to practice both/and rather than either/or thinking. Few situations are clearly black or white.

Pause and Ponder: *What are you taking away from this discussion of creating a conscious relationship?*

A Piece of the Puzzle

A relationship is an organic entity with a life of its own. If not nurtured, it will die. A conscious relationship provides an avenue for partners to heal psychic wounds and to pursue and experience unconditional love. Practicing loving kindness results in trust, a key component of a healthy relationship.

Loving Communication

One divorce coach/consultant found lack of communication skills to be one of three reasons people divorce. The other two are laziness and expectations that don't align with reality.

This acronym for love that I created for the class that led to writing this book provides a framework for the discussion of loving communication.

Listen

Observe

Value

Encourage

In *The 7 Habits of Highly Effective People,* Stephen Covey proclaimed that communication is the most important skill in life.[33] In discussing his fifth habit, "Seek first to understand, then to be understood," Covey contends that empathic listening requires a major paradigm shift from our egocentric mind. In other words, we must endeavor to understand where the other person is coming from. In the process, our partners feel valued and encouraged to share their experiences and be themselves without pretending to be who the listener wants them to be. Cut to its core, loving communication involves conscious, empathic listening that is free of judgments. Observing requires the ability to understand others, including non-verbal cues, without putting them in a box based on expectations or categories. The practice of "listening, observing, valuing, and encouraging another" runs counter to the self-absorbed orientation of the egoic mind.

Take a moment to ponder the title of Matt Kahn's profound book, *Whatever Arises, Love That.*[34] In any given interaction, we have a choice. We can use the reactive mind state to judge a

---

33 Covey, Stephen, *The Seven Habits of Highly Effective People* (New York: Simon &Shuster Fireside, 1989)

34 Khan, *op. cit.*

statement and mentally prepare a rebuttal, or we can be open to understand and accept the other person's reality. It's clear which will result in loving communication. In this context, it's good to avoid "why" responses when communicating. "Why" tends to question the other person's motive and may convey a judgment in the sense of "Where in the world are *you* coming from?" It's better to say: "I don't understand, please say more."

Recognizing our propensity to react from fear or anger and to feed our egoic minds, to communicate lovingly we must develop a *pause button* and a filter system. We have all heard the advice: "Think before you speak." Before speaking, pause and ask yourself these three questions: Is what I am going to say true? Is it necessary? Is it kind?

Words of affirmation come naturally when we accept the realities in life as Matt Kahn suggests. Recalling our earlier discussion of the words "like" and "dislike," the latter can be a killer. If "I don't like" becomes a mantra, you may want to seek professional help. Words of affirmation lubricate a growing, healthy relationship. We all have self-doubts and crave appreciation. As you interact with your partner, express appreciation for words or acts that you value. Conflicts are inevitable in relationships. When they can't be resolved with words, follow this advice I received in a couples' workshop: Employ the wisdom of the bodies by getting them together; being naked works best.

Beware of the tendency to inject humor into a situation. Media sage Marshall McLuhan proclaimed, "Jokes are grievances." An online search for McLuhan's wisdom also found these gems:

"A point of view can be a dangerous luxury when substituted for insight and understanding."

"Most of our assumptions have outlived their usefulness."[35]

On the other hand, as long as it doesn't hurt the other person or leave him/her feeling not being taken seriously, humor can prevent a relationship from becoming too serious. We all benefit from having levity in our lives and emoting through laughing.

Pause and Ponder: *What are you taking away from this discussion of loving communication?*

A Piece of the Puzzle

"Stop. Look. Listen"—-the caution at a railroad crossing is a good metaphor for loving communication, which is critical to creating and maintaining a loving relationship. Beware of the reactive mind and create a pause button to practice thinking before speaking. Have awareness of the impact that what you are about to say may have on your partner. Don't complain—compliment.

Breaking Through to Love

Searching for self-understanding and self-acceptance has been a decades-long journey for me. During my forties, I found a psychotherapist named Deborah who did not take my insurance. When I asked her why I should spend thousands of dollars working with her, Deborah said something profound: "So you can be happy in your old age." Deborah was right. Do I still have my stuff? Of course. But increasingly, I see it for what it is—fleeting thoughts and feelings that I know will fade away if I don't create a sense of "I am" out of them. As Deborah predicted,

---

35 McLuhan quotes online.

I'm happier in my eighties than I have ever been before in my life.

As our emphasis shifts from the brain to the heart, we encounter terms like "coldhearted," "have a heart," "he/she is all heart," "a heart of steel," "warmhearted," "sweetheart," and "heartless"—all parts of our everyday language. They connote loving kindness, or the lack thereof. And then there is Valentine's Day, of course, where the heart is a symbol of affection and love. As one's heart opens, loving thoughts and feelings lead to loving behavior. As the mind is a metaphor for thinking, the heart is a metaphor for the realm of feelings—energy flows in the body.

Once again, recall that your journey to learning and practicing unconditional love began by following the advice of the 13th Century Persian poet and Sufi mystic Rumi: "Your task is not to seek for love, but merely to seek and find the barriers within yourself that you have built up against love."[36] In other words, each of us must identify, acknowledge, and let go of our unique pattern of what might be called our *brokenness*. Thinking about this process, the analogy to a vacuum cleaner popped up in my mind one morning. As the debris of life is vacuumed away, the loving mystical mind state we were born with can slowly reemerge.

How to make the transition from the primal, reactive, and rational mind states to the mystical mind, is a key question. Of the myriad paths I have explored, I have benefited greatly from these three.

1.   *Psychotherapy* involves uncovering one's conditioning or brokenness in individual or group sessions with a

---

36 Rumi, *op. cit.*

skilled therapist. As noted earlier, from my experience, "talk therapy" focuses largely on the mind at the expense of the body and feelings.

2. *Twelve Step Recovery Work* begins when someone admits that he/she is powerless over dependence on a substance, childhood conditioning, or a relationship. And, feeling powerless, one's life has become unmanageable.

3. In Buddhism, *Insight Meditation* helps one become aware of the pain and suffering that results from conditioning and life circumstances. As a process of observing the mind, "What is this?" is a key question during the meditation process.

Psychotherapy, twelve-step recovery work, and insight meditation all deal with uncovering dukkha, a Buddhist term meaning "suffering, unsatisfactoriness, anxiety, and stress." In addition to gaining freedom from conditioning and craving that leads to suffering, one of the goals of Buddhist practice is to awaken to a new, yet old, reality, our Buddha nature, by pursuing the Dharma path to enlightenment. Like the Buddha, we all have the potential to regain the loving hearts we were born with and to rise above our egoic mind state. In addition to letting go of limiting habitual mind patterns and accepting ourselves, we can learn to accept and love those around us and maybe a special person.

Pause and Ponder: *What are you taking away from this discussion of breaking through to love?*

A Piece of the Puzzle

Adopt a practice to heal from your brokenness. Psychotherapy, twelve-step recovery work, and Buddhist insight meditation provide some options.

Be Here Now

The term "be here now" is attributed to a 1971 book of that name by Ram Das. *Mindfulness* is another name for this philosophy. But what does it mean to *be mindful*? Is it the opposite of being unconscious? And what do the words "*be, here, and now*" mean?

In *Alone with Others,* Buddhist scholar Stephen Batchelor makes a distinction between two verbs, "to be" and "to have," and contends that "having" is experienced on an ever-receding horizontal plane.[37] Some people are never satisfied and always want to have more. Batchelor contends that the primary purpose of Buddhist dharma practice is to reestablish the *consciousness of being* we were born with. In contrast to horizontal, *being* is felt in its vertical depths, what Tillich named the ground of our being.

Because our minds have a tendency to be anywhere but *here* in the present moment, mindfulness is the essence of the *being* mode of living. In *Wherever You Go, There You Are,* Jon Kabat-Zinn discusses the tendency of our minds to go on automatic pilot and actually lose touch with the only time we actually have to live, and that, like a garden that needs to be weeded, *being* mindful of the present moment needs to be cultivated.[38]

---

37 Batchelor, *Alone with Others,* op. cit.

38 Kabat-Zinn, *op. cit.*

Pause and Ponder: *How often are you fully present?*

Equanimity—calmness in difficult situations—is central to Buddhist practice. The Buddha urged his disciples to cultivate the ability to perceive conditions clearly without being caught up in them. Cultivating this skill allows one to remain involved in the world while maintaining a sense of detachment and peace. Being fully mindful of the realities of the present moment, which includes the needs of others, requires compassion.

The Power of Now, a profound book by Eckhart Tolle published in 1999, expanded on the mindfulness theme.[39] In essence, Tolle argues that the only time we have is *now.* Unfortunately, the human mind tends to be overwhelmed with regrets about the past and fear of the future. In other words, it struggles to be in the present moment.

A Piece of the Puzzle

Love is found at our deepest, most conscious level of being and flourishes in the present moment.

I and Thou: Getting from I to We

For the first nine months of life, infants are one with their mothers in utero. But as infants grow, separation occurs as a sense of "I" develops. For many children in our culture, this is a traumatic break. But for the fortunate infants with loving mothers who make bonding with their child a priority, the break from oneness is more natural. Central to the Buddhist dharma teaching is the idea that oneness is not a goal; it is

---

39 Tolle, Eckhart, *The Power of Now* (Novato, CA: New World Library, 1999).

the reality of life. Equality, regardless of race or nationality, is oneness. Compassion for those in need is oneness. It connotes empathy for all others.

The German language has two words for *you*: *"sie"* and *"du."* The latter is reserved for those with whom one feels a special connection. Two people who have evolved into love consciousness become a "we" without losing their individual identities. Martin Buber termed this connection "*I and Thou.*"[40]

Creating oneness in a loving relationship begins when both partners follow the wisdom of Rumi. As each partner begins to identify and let go of their individual blocks to love; a new sense of oneness (a new "we" perspective) can emerge. In this process, the wisdom of Viktor Frankl comes into play: "The loving person enables the beloved person to actualize [his/her] potentialities." Over time, the duality of "I" thinking and speaking fades away and a sense of oneness replaces it. However, this does not mean that either party loses his/her individuality. Quite the opposite. The partner's support of each other to achieve their individual potentials becomes an emphasis of the relationship. For some, this may happen intuitively. However, in our egocentric culture, most of us must learn and practice this new perspective.

In *Alone with Others,* Bachelor makes a distinction between *inauthentic* "being with others" motivated by self-interest and *authentic* being with others—seeing and accepting others as they are—equally sentient beings who are hoping and fearing, loving and hating, living and dying. Batchelor's thinking is consistent with Martin Buber's concept of an *I-It*

---

40 Buber, Martin, *I and Thou* (New York: Simon and Schuster Touchstone Book, 1970).

relationship, where the *other* is viewed as an object to satisfy selfish needs.

According to Batchelor, if self-interest is our steady state, a commitment and work to achieve authentic being-with-others is required. In Buddhist terms, we achieve authentic "being with others" by cultivating loving kindness and generosity. Batchelor prescribes a sustained contemplation of the equality of self and others which descends to a depth at which we suddenly touch the essential reality that we are one with others.[41] This realization that we are connected is as essential to our well-being as a mother's love is essential to an infant. At eighty-seven, living with Mary Anne is essential to my well-being. I believe the same is true for her. We are blessed to be going through the isolation of the coronavirus pandemic together.

This radical change of orientation from "I" to "we" is not a linear process. You will know you have arrived when trust develops to the point where fear gives way to a love comparable to a mother's love for her infant child. Projections and unmet expectations are part of the human condition. The difference is that "we" partners talk about what is going on. Every evolving, loving relationship requires acceptance of differences and adjustments to them.

Becoming a *We*

Being in a relationship with Mary Anne is changing me. However, continuing to be aware of my unique barriers to love is an ongoing process. Have I been able to apply insights from "Learning to Love" to my own life? Am I more conscious than I was when I met Mary Anne and we began this learning

---

41 Batchelor, *Alone With Others, op. cit.*

adventure during the eighth decade of my life? My unqualified answer to these questions is YES. Mary Anne and I are evolving into a "*we*."

- *We* accept each other for who we are.
- *We* share similar values and do our best to live by them.
- *We* value each other's unique talents and experiences which contribute to the richness of our relationship.
- *We* take time each day to ponder and verbalize our many blessings, the biggest being the sharing of our "golden years" together.
- When criticisms come to mind, *we* have learned to engage our pause buttons and take time to discuss the situation.
- *We* take daily walks hand-in-hand.
- *We* watch the PBS news summary sitting on our love seat.
- *We* share meal preparation and cleaning up.
- Our spacious apartment gives us privacy when *we* desire it.
- Most mornings, *we* spend quality time together before and after breakfast.
- Hugs are an important part of *our* days.
- To stay fit as *we* approach our nineties, yoga stretching is a part of our days.
- Keeping in touch with family is important to both of us and adds richness to our lives.

- *We* are blessed to know another couple we enjoy spending time with.

Having a happy, upbeat partner in Mary Anne is a new experience and blessing for me. I can't imagine a better life than I have right now. What have Mary Anne and I learned as we walk together on the journey of learning to love? At our core, we are love, and therefore, we are lovable. Self-acceptance and empathy for others are the core attributes of learning to love.

I'm going to end with a dream and my interpretation of it. In the dream, several of us have rented a cottage for a week. When we get there, we find that a man is occupying one of the bedrooms. I ask him to leave, which he does. Having learned that every aspect of a dream is a part of me, I pondered who the intruder into the serenity of my vacation might be. I concluded that he represents my self-absorbed mind. The good news is that I sent him packing in my dream. Letting go of my egoic mind allows me to create a sense of oneness—an *"I-Thou"* relationship with Mary Anne and loving connections with my children. I wish doing so was as easy as it was in my dream.

A Piece of the Puzzle

As you let go of your individual blocks to love, a new sense of oneness (a "we" perspective) can emerge as an "I-Thou" relationship.

Learning to Love: Summing It Up

The ability to give and receive love—to be connected— is our birthright as human beings. At birth, our hearts are completely open. Look at an infant for proof of this assertion.

Quoting from the book of Matthew, Jesus invited a little child to stand among the gathering, and said, "Unless you change and become like little children, you cannot enter the kingdom of heaven." This biblical quote is consistent with my belief that we are born with pure love.

As a child grows, two things happen. First, the child's wings get clipped to make him/her acceptable to the family, schools, and community (which may include a religion). Using the words of the Toltec of Mexico, we become domesticated. We learn what behavior is acceptable. In the process, our minds supersede our hearts—the realm of feelings and love—and, over time, we build a shell around our hearts. Second, we develop a sense of self and the belief that this fabrication, called the egoic mind by Eckhart Tolle, is who we really are. This process of individuation to create a unique identity is a lifelong pursuit. However, there are many pitfalls along the way. As our demons, addictions, and repressed emotions arise, our minds have a tendency to identify with them. When they arise, we must recognize them as fleeting experiences that will go away as long as we don't create a sense of "I am" out of them.

At some point, we may recognize that something important—love—is missing from our lives. At that point, we begin to question the identity our mind and our fears have created; using a colloquial term, we begin to look at "our stuff." We search for a deeper understanding of who we are at our core—the authentic loving self that is our birthright. We let go of "that's just the way I am" thinking and replace it with "I'm not the same person I was a year ago or a decade ago, and I can continue to change who I am."

Connecting with a significant other is an avenue for healing the human tendency to be self-absorbed. However, chances are you have never learned how to love—to reclaim your birthright. Let's recall the formula to (re)learn to love.

Listen

Observe

Value

Encourage

These are skills each of us can learn; they are not about our ego. Is this a formula to live happily ever after? Hardly. *A Course in Miracles* proclaimed: "Love brings up everything unlike itself for the purpose of healing and release." Our "stuff," whether wounds from childhood or from a previous relationship, will come up in a new relationship. Wounds, if ignored, are likely to fester. However, if issues are confronted with honesty, courage, compassion, and open communication, the new relationship has a good chance to thrive.

As you embark on this journey, your egoic mind will continue to fight for dominance. You will be confronted with your unique demons and addictions. Unwanted feelings will continue to arise. However, your better understanding of the human condition will give you a wiser perspective to recognize that these thoughts and feelings are not who you are. As you nurture your love intelligence, your love consciousness will grow through an intuitive, mystical process. Your Buddha nature or Christ consciousness will emerge.

As you become a more loving person, never forget *how* you get to Carnegie Hall. A commitment to practice loving kindness will be the key to living a richer, fuller, more meaningful life. A sense of "we" will emerge and grow when a partner joins you in a conscious, loving relationship.

Chapter 6:

Creating Your Unique Roadmap to Love

The following are pieces of the *Learning to Love* puzzle that summarize Chapter 5:

1. Rumi: "Your task is not to seek for love, but merely to seek and find the barriers within yourself that you have built up against it."

2. The self-absorbed mind represents the greatest barrier to love.

3. Because the reactive mind state controls most of our moment-to-moment responses to events, fears from the past can constitute a fundamental barrier to giving and receiving love.

4. Love consciousness grows as we get in touch with the purity of our nature at birth.

5. "Awakening" is the Buddhist term for accessing this love consciousness.

6. While you may not like a situation, accept its reality and benefit from what it has to teach you.

7. To change your situation in the future, use the *Serenity Prayer*.

8. Who we are results from interactions between our DNA and our life experiences—our nature and our nurture.

9.   Like a lobster, we develop shells to protect us.

10. Loving relationships have the capacity to heal our wounds and dissolve our shells.

11. As humans, we experience a dark side, which is the antithesis of love.

12. Uncomfortable thoughts and feelings will fade away if we don't create a sense of self out of them.

13. Loving communication is critical to creating and maintaining a loving relationship.

14. Loving relationships have the capacity to heal our psychic wounds.

15. All of us are addicted to some substance or belief.

16. Meaningful change results from owning the addiction and making a commitment to overcome it with the guidance of our higher power.

17. Our values determine how we use our time and resources; generosity and greed are polar opposites.

18. Before we can change our values, we must recognize and question the ones that don't serve us in learning to love.

19. We must become conscious of our unique repressed emotions which create barriers to love.

20. Emoting is the only way to release feelings and emotions like sadness, joy, and anger.

21. When your demons arise, learn from them.

22. Become aware of your internal conflicts and have the courage to talk to your partner about what is going on within you.

23. Your partner is also experiencing his/her tension of the opposites.

24. Having a partner who is committed to personal growth is critical to the process of creating a loving relationship.

25. As it requires a conscious effort and time to understand yourself, a similar conscious effort must be made to know your partner's potential.

26. Your love can enable your partner to reach his/her potential.

27. A relationship is an organic entity with a life of its own. If not nurtured, it will die.

28. Practicing loving kindness results in trust, a key component of a healthy relationship.

29. A conscious, loving relationship provides an avenue for partners to heal psychic wounds.

30. "Stop. Look. Listen"—the cautionary warning at a railroad crossing, is a good metaphor for loving communication.

31. Beware of your reactive mind and create a pause button to practice thinking before speaking.

32. Be aware of the impact that what you are about to say may have on your partner.

33. Accentuate the positive. Don't complain—compliment.

34. When upsets occur, talk about them. Don't let them accumulate until you explode in anger.

35. We live moment-to-moment. Accepting the reality of each moment and loving it works better than denying it.

36. Instead of mentally rehashing the past or worrying about the future, "be here now."

37. Your presence is your greatest gift to another.

38. Letting go of your individual blocks to love permits a new sense of oneness (of "we") to surface.

39. This sense of oneness can morph into an "I-Thou" relationship.

Reading this book, you have learned a lot about me and my search for love, and finding it. What have you learned about yourself that you will take away from the book? If you have a desire to change and to create a loving relationship, recognizing your barriers to love is the starting point. Overcoming these barriers will allow you to uncover the loving nature you were born with. Now it's time to take a brief personal inventory of your unique barriers to love. Circle the numbers of each of the following statements that describe you. Be honest with yourself.

1. To a great extent, I tend to be self-absorbed.

2. In intimate situations, my protective shell is pretty thick.

3. In a relationship, I tend to be codependent.

4. Being fully present in the moment is not easy for me.

5. I often identify (create a sense of "I am") with my demons.

6. Knowing what I'm feeling is difficult for me.

7. Expressing emotions is also difficult for me.

8. I infrequently use my pause button to think before speaking.

9. It's not easy for me to share my upsets with others.

10. I tend to be more negative than positive.

11. Having empathy for others is difficult for me.

12. I sometimes complain and blame other people.

13. I tend to be critical.

14. I like to control situations.

15. I tend to be impatient.

Drawing on the items you have circled on the above list of fifteen barriers, make a list of your unique barriers. Your list may include other barriers not on the list.

Write a vision statement based upon the changes you want to make. Who do you want to become? Then, using the barriers you circled, put them in a sequential order to create a roadmap of changes you plan to make.

Where are you on your roadmap? What is the next stop on your journey? Be specific.

Conclusion

Our commitment to change is critical to personal growth. Although our thoughts and feelings may resist change, we can always change our behavior. As knee-jerk reactions arise, we can hit our pause button. Rather than reacting unconsciously, we can use our rational mind to choose loving responses. We can cultivate our mystical mind to activate our intuition, our deeper knowledge. Although enlightenment is a worthy goal, we are fortunate if we experience occasional flashes of it—moments when our ego has retreated completely into the background. These are periods of awakening to the reality of oneness, the unity of all life. Develop a sense of "we" with other human beings and with the natural world. Finally, adopt and cultivate generosity as your North Star. When love prevails, anything is possible. I wish you well on your journey. To create a loving relationship in your life, the time to begin is ***now.***

Final Pause and Ponder: *These two questions were posed at the end of the introduction. Is it possible to learn to love? If one does learn to love, will he/she be happy? Having read the book, how would you answer these two questions now?*

Acknowledgments

Like producing a motion picture, writing a book is a process of reduction—more is left on the cutting room floor than what makes its way into the final product. The process of writing *Learning to Love Later in Life* began more than fifteen years ago with the title *Living Among the Dead: A Memoir by the Undertaker's Second Son.*

After my divorce, when I was a student in a program to become an interfaith chaplain the seeds for writing a memoir were planted. Looking back, this program, which I never finished, laid the foundation for the next twenty years of my life. I'm indebted to Rev. Jacob Watson, the founder of the Chaplaincy Institute of Maine, for including two exercises that changed my life. The first was a shamanic journey to find my totem animal, which turned out to be a squirrel. The second was proprioceptive writing—a method for exploring the mind through writing. These exercises opened the door into my unconscious mind. I know this because after the exercises, I was waking up in the middle of the night with memories and insights into my life. After initially resisting the process, I surrendered to it and began taking notes, which I later developed into my memoir. My first editor was Kate Kaminski, a resident of Maine, where I was living at the time. My second editor was Kathleen Spivack in Massachusetts. Kathleen and Kate, thank you for guiding me and encouraging my "muse."

When the memoir was finished, my son-in-law, Basil Steele, read and gave me feedback on the manuscript. I then placed my memoir in a blue binder and put the project on the back burner. As you have read, my life changed when I met Mary Anne Multer and we decided it was time to learn to love. This led to offering "Learning to Love" as a class in the Osher Lifelong Learning Institute at the University of Delaware. After Mary Anne and I offered the class twice, I decided to write this book based on the research I had done to develop the class. My daughters, Cindy and Cathy, my granddaughter, Anya, and Basil Steele read versions of the manuscript. In addition to family members, I shared my writing with Stephanie Iacovelli, Mary Anne's daughter, and Anne Fossler, a friend at Osher. All offered the words of encouragement an author requires and constructive feedback. My thanks to all of you.

At that point, I decided that I needed a skilled editor. An online search identified Ann Murphy, who lives fifteen minutes away. Ann made two important contributions that dramatically altered the character of the book. She encouraged me to incorporate my memoir into the story. She also told me that the manuscript reads too much like a textbook. When he read the manuscript, Bob Kaiser, my freshman college roommate, echoed Ann's insight. Thank you, Ann, for initiating a transformation of the manuscript.

With much of what I have written knee-deep on the "cutting room" floor, I decided it was time to find a publisher and recognized that I needed another experienced editor to guide the way. By good fortune, I found Robin Hill-Page Glanden, who offered valuable suggestions to tighten the manuscript, and edited it for publication. Thank you, Robin, for guiding me on the journey from writing to publishing.

After looking at self-publishing companies, my friend, Tara Tieman, told me about BookBaby. My contact person at BookBaby is Avery Bacchues who has ably guided me through the process of creating a finished book, and my thanks to his colleagues who have edited the manuscript, formatted the text, and designed the cover..

I also want to recognize Dr. Jay Jemail, the last of my psychotherapists, for introducing me to the "tension of the opposites" concept and my friend, Steve Johnson, for helping me understand the importance of "nature *and* nurture". Steve also read many chapters of the evolving manuscript and gave me valuable feedback. Bob Bercaw, a Science of Mind practitioner, taught me about the levels of consciousness in a short course that Mary Anne and I attended at Awakened Heart Spiritual Center in Wilmington, Delaware. Jay, Steve, and Bob, thank you for introducing me to these important concepts as I was learning to love and writing about it.

Had Mary Anne Multer not walked into my life and become my partner, this book would not have been written. As I was writing, Mary Anne read and critiqued my daily flow of words. As in life, Mary Anne was my partner in completing this book by carefully editing and proofreading the final copy. Her insights resulted in a clearer, more readable book. Thank you, Mary Anne.

Readers of the book may not agree with everything I have written about the process of learning to love. Bear in mind that this is a memoir, not a textbook. With Mary Anne as my partner, what I have written is working for us. Now in our eighties, we are enjoying the love that we have found.